THE SHATTERED PEARL

D1056721

by

Sara L. Armstrong

ISBN-13: 978-0615563664 (Sara L. Armstrong Enterprises)

*To my daughter, son and grandchildren,
so that you may know your history*

*To my late husband Bob, in appreciation for his
love, care and support*

Prologue

I'm was not quite sure what awakened me that night - - Perhaps the sound of tires on the gravel in the driveway, or maybe some sixth sense told me that danger might be near.

I lay very still for a moment straining to hear. The familiar sounds of the East African night filled the room; the rhythmic chirping of insects, the mournful wail of night birds, the soft rustle of fronds of the banana trees stirred by the gentle night breeze. But there was another sound, the quiet, steady hum of a car engine.

I slid out of bed and crawled along next to the wall until I was under the open window. Slowly raising my head, I chanced a look outside. The moon shown brightly in the clear East African sky and I could see the Land Rover in the driveway. Three men sat inside talking.

Who were they? Who had they come for? Would they kill my children, or me? Would we disappear as so many had before? Tears of fear and anger began to flow. Why did we have to live like this? I didn't know how much more I could take. Please God, help us to get out.

Chapter 1

Portraits in Black and Whites

He cried. In our twenty-one years together I never saw him cry - - even when we buried his brother and his father. But on that day the most exciting day of my life, my father cried. His head moved slowly from left to right as though to say, "No. It can't be true. She can't be leaving." The light brown summer straw hat he wore was slightly askew, and when he removed it, to dab at his eyes and blow his nose, it ruffled his wavy, gray hair which he wore pulled straight back and molded to the scalp.

My mother stood with her usual stiff schoolteacher posture, a death grip on my hand. Her brown eyes stared at me from her chocolate brown face. They reflected an ever-changing mixture of pride, love, sadness and longing. I wondered what she was feeling. Envy? Regret? Her dreams of being a missionary in Africa had been stifled. My grandfather refused to let her go. And now, forty years later, her daughter, her only child was going to Africa in the Peace Corps.

Travelers bustled by as we stood at the departure gate in O'Hare Airport that September day in 1966. The

2

loudspeaker barked out the last call for my flight to New York and the moment of final umbilical and paternal separation was at hand.

"Take care of yourself, Piggy," my father croaked. The use of his special name for me brought comfort rather than embarrassment. "Remember, we are here if you need us," he said, giving me one final short but intense bear hug.

In her most rounded and pear shaped tones my mother said, "You know how to act. Remember who you are and how you were raised."

"I'll call you as soon as I get there," I interjected before I could be instructed to do so. Giving my mother a brief embrace, I hurried down the walkway to the plane.

A sense of freedom filled my heart. For the first time in my life I was truly on my own. Growing up as an only child born to parents in their forties came with certain perks; but there were drawbacks. For instance the matter of being named after my mother. She said, "This was my only chance to name a child after me; so I took it." Because having two Sara Louise McWrights in the family was confusing, and due to an unfortunate remark by my cousin, "She's as sweet as pie," I became know as Sweetie Pie.

As the plane lifted off and the familiar skyline of

3

my native Chicago disappeared under the clouds, excitement and anticipation rapidly turned to feelings of inadequacy and panic. What did I think I was doing? Leaving a perfectly good home, with loving parents and a cute nickname and going out into the big cold world? Was I crazy? No. I might be stifled, smothered and bored, but not crazy.

I am a living experiment in child rearing. My parents believed that a healthy combination of discipline, love and exposure to all things intellectual would produce a happy and well-balanced human being. And they were right, sort of. Love abounded in my life. I cannot recall ever being left with a babysitter. Wherever my parents went, I went. Being a well-disciplined and obedient child, I was a pleasure to have around. Because I kept quiet and amused myself without adult intervention, my ears developed radar for intercepting bits of information and gossip. I didn't always understand what I heard, but I knew it was important.

Books, music, TV and news filled our home. My parents read the newspaper every day. We watched the national and local news as we ate dinner. My father, who only finished the eighth grade in his native Mississippi, read avidly and could hold his own in a conversation about boxing or the causes of World War II. He taught me the basics of football and baseball and the words to Guy Lombardo songs.

I endured piano and violin lessons, enjoyed Young People's Concerts at Orchestra Hall where I was introduced to *Peter and the Wolf*, and *The Nutcracker Suite*. I listened to Fibber McGee and Molly on the radio and watched Lucy, Ed Sullivan and the Hallmark Hall of Fame on TV. I was as well rounded as a Hoola Hoop.

Formal education fell to my mother. She was one of twelve children raised in an Alabama family that valued education. After receiving her teaching certificate, she spent many years in rural areas using creative methods to teach under difficult circumstances. This was not a woman who would believe the dog ate your homework. I was groomed to excel. Reading by age four with a vocabulary far beyond my years, I skipped two grades in elementary school and at the tender age of twelve was thrust into high school.

Here was the rub: While delighting adults and feeling comfortable in their presence, rapport with my own age group was difficult. Because they were older, everyone else in high school could do things I couldn't. My skirts were longer, my shoes less stylish and my parents dropped me off and picked me up from every party; social suicide. Even after graduation, my parents didn't feel that a sixteen-year-old could handle college campus life. So I lived at home and took the bus to Roosevelt University in downtown Chicago.

Determined to break free, after graduation from college, I used a sophisticated job search technique. I wrote a letter to the Air Force and one to the Peace Corps. Whoever answered me first would get me. The Peace Corps won. Originally, I was scheduled to go to Tunisia in North Africa as a Health Care Worker, but my inability to pass an organic chemistry course necessitated attending summer school. The Peace Corps, however, still found me worthy and reassigned me to an education project in Uganda, East Africa.

I didn't know where Uganda was until I located it in the atlas. Uganda is west of Kenya, and east of what was then known as Zaire (formerly know as the Belgian Congo, and now known as the Peoples Republic of the Congo). The encyclopedia revealed little else except that Uganda is about the same size as Oregon produces great coffee, and that the headwaters of the Nile River could be found there. My assignment to teach in secondary school (roughly equivalent to high school) delighted my mother. Little Sara fulfills her destiny and follows in Big Sara's footsteps. The Peace Corps only required that the trainees for this project have a Bachelors Degree. Teaching experience was helpful but not mandatory. With my degree in Microbiology and minor in Chemistry, I would most certainly teach science. My original intention in entering science was job security. The Russians beat the United States into space and now the push was to catch up. I figured that science was my ticket to a great job and an opportunity to find a cure for cancer in my spare time. I really wanted to study drama or writing but no child of Sara and Edward McWright could fritter her time away in such foolish pursuits.

The plane trip was uneventful. After landing, I moved through the terminal with an air of confidence that I truly did not feel. My mother taught me that if you look like you are alert and know what you are doing, even if you don't, you won't get your purse snatched or be otherwise victimized. This seemed a perfect time to test her theory. I found my luggage and secured a taxi without incident and said with as sophisticated an air as I could muster, "Paris Hotel, 752 West End Avenue."

New York City rolled past the taxicab window. Skyscrapers where captains of commerce and industry fueled the American economy; neon lights advertising cigarettes, Broadway plays and beer; graffiti-covered walls marking gang territory. I knew all about gangs. After all I saw *West Side Story* six times. The kid was loose in New York. Training promised to be as great an adventure as going to Africa.

The Paris Hotel bordered on the edge of seediness. It retained remnants of days gone by when it had been chic and fashionable. But now the carpet was worn in spots, the elevator creaked, and the towels were beginning to ravel around the edges. As each of the 150 trainees arrived, they were assigned a room, and directed to the mezzanine where Peace Corps staff welcomed them with forms, reading material and schedules.

My room was non-descript, but to me it was heaven. It had a double bed, small bathroom and even a tiny refrigerator. And best of all it was mine - - just mine. I could come and go as I pleased. I could stay out late and walk on the wild side. Free at last.

After settling in, I went down to the mezzanine to pick up training information. In the midst of gathering piles of paper a voice behind me said "It sure is a lot of stuff isn't it?" I had no doubt that the owner was female and from the South. I turned to face her and looked into smiling brown eyes. She wore simple black frame glasses and stood about my height of 5'4", maybe a little taller. Her brown hair was teased in a soft bouffant style.

"Yes, it sure is," I replied. "My name is Sara."

"My name is Nadine[1]," she answered. We shook hands awkwardly

trying not to drop our load of books and papers. As we continued down the line of tables, I found that Nadine was from a small town in Georgia. Her degree was in English, and she was already teaching in North Carolina when she decided to join the Peace Corps. Both of us were assigned to Uganda.

Nadine asked if I would walk with her to dinner at a nearby cafeteria where the trainees were to eat that evening. We agreed to meet in the lobby later. As Nadine walked away, I mused, "Why would a white girl from North Carolina want to go to Africa?"

My reaction surprised me a little. My upbringing was what I considered liberal. I was taught to judge everyone by their actions not their color. But I was steeped in the realities of what it meant to be black in America. It meant always being a little bit better than whites to get the same position. It meant never acting "typical", as my

---

[1] Some names have been changed in the interest of privacy.

mother would say. That meant not being loud or boisterous around whites so that they wouldn't think you fit the stereotype. I could hear my mother's constant admonition to me whenever I left the house "Act your age and not your color." Your shoes must be shined, your hair in place and your underwear clean. Never be loud, never be ignorant, and never let them see you sweat.

I grew up with stories of the victimization and brutalization of black people. My father and his family were run out of Mississippi when he was eighteen because my grandfather tried to organize the tenant farmers. My mother taught school for months during the Depression without being paid, while the white teachers never missed a paycheck. Being black in America, I had experienced my share of direct and indirect racism. I never marched or picketed, but my dedication to the civil rights movement was deep. So I found myself a little apprehensive about going to dinner with a white southerner, even a fellow Peace Corps trainee.

As we strolled along in the twilight and talked I found that Nadine, like me, was looking for a way to have some adventure and help someone at the same time. Nadine was a trained teacher with a degree in education. As we ate, we talked about family, fears, hopes, and

10

expectations. Honesty and genuine warmth radiated from her smile. She could laugh at herself and laugh with others. I had made my first Peace Corps friend.

The next morning training began at Columbia University, a short bus ride from the hotel. Nadine and I arrived early and took seats down front in the huge tiered lecture hall. The room filled quickly and when the session began, I tried to survey the group of 150 as unobtrusively as I could. A group of black men sat nearby speaking in a language I didn't understand. My suspicions were confirmed when they were introduced as our language instructors. As I studied the remaining people in the room, my heart rate doubled and my stomach turned. I was the only black trainee. I wanted to leave. I wanted to scream. I wanted my Mommy.

I had been the only black in a class at college or a seminar or a weekend retreat. But this was for three months, day in and day out. Why, if we were assigned to the same school in Uganda, I might even end up having one of these people as a roommate. My mind ran amuck. The significance of my situation took on global implications. It was 1966, in the midst of the civil rights movement, and I alone carried the fate of my entire race on my shoulders. For surely if I failed, the future of blacks in the Peace

Corps was bleak. I wanted my Mommy.

Any notion that my fellow trainees were oblivious to the situation was soon dispelled. Whenever a speaker would say African, Negro, or black, 149 pairs of eyes stared at me. I didn't know whether to raise my fist and shout "Black Power", or ask everyone to join hands, sway from side to side and sing *We Shall Overcome.*

During the first break I hurried to the bathroom, splashed water on my face and sought the solitude of a toilet cubicle to compose myself. After taking a few deep breaths and determining that I wasn't going to lose my breakfast, I resolved that I could handle this situation and walked out of the stall and into the hallway renewed and steely in my determination. That was when I saw him coming toward me. I had met him many times before. Sometimes he is a she; old, young, rich, poor, he came in many forms. The one distinguishing characteristic was that if you were the only member of a minority in a group, this person, "Larry, I'm Going to Show Everyone I'm a Liberal", would find you.

He worked his way through the crowd with his eyes fixed on me like Sylvester stalking Tweety. His face fixed in a wide, forced smile and his hand poised either to shake mine or pat me on the head.

"Hi, there," he boomed. "My name is Larry." Or whatever; I really don't remember.

"Hi, I'm Sara," I replied through clenched teeth.

"I saw you in there, and just wanted to introduce myself," he explained.

I thanked him and asked the standard questions about home state, school and Peace Corps destination. To my great relief he was going to Kenya.

As the group began to file back into the classroom, he dropped his final pearl of patronization. "I just want you to know that I'm really glad that you are here. I don't have any problem with it at all. In fact, my cousin married a West Indian man and my family just loves him."

I wanted to say, "I'm sure he's thrilled with you, too," but decided that sarcasm at this point wasn't wise. Smiling politely and mumbling an insincere, "Nice to meet you", and "See you later", I returned to my seat.

I pondered as I sat there, Why was I alone? Where were the other black trainees? Maybe they were involved in the civil rights struggle. Maybe they were taking advantage of the new opportunities that were available. Maybe no serious efforts were being made to recruit minorities. For whatever reason, it struck me as odd that white Americans were more interested in going to Africa than black Americans.

Was something wrong with me? Was I different from other blacks? Had my rather sheltered upbringing made me think or act differently from others of my race? None of that was relevant. I was there. I wasn't going home and everyone, including me, would just have to cope.

The trainees ranged in age from twenty-one to thirty- married couples, Jews, Catholic, Baptists and two trainees in their seventies. Every area of the United States was represented, as were Ivy League schools, state universities and smaller liberal arts or church affiliated schools. Majors ranged from the standards like English, Biology, and Sociology to the more eclectic such as French Literature, Biochemistry, and Anthropology.

Surprisingly, at least for me, a significant number of the trainees came from affluent backgrounds. They had attended Ivy League and exclusive private colleges, and many expressed a need to get out and learn about the real world.

The training schedule varied daily. From 8:30 a.m. to
4:30 p.m. we attended structured activities. Classroom teaching techniques were reviewed. We scrutinized the syllabi used in East Africa. East African history and

culture were discussed in detail. Former Peace Corps Volunteers (PCVs), college professors, psychologists and a variety of experts facilitated these sessions. Some were enjoyable, others we just endured. By the eleventh week of training, each trainee was required to prepare a research paper on some aspect of Africa. I cannot remember on what I wrote the paper or what grade, if any, I received.

Female trainees learned netball and male trainees learned soccer, both to promote physical fitness and be more versatile as members of a school faculty. As trainees we undertook our own fitness program. We walked from the hotel at 97th Street to Columbia at 120th Street and back again in the evening. The weather didn't really bother us. Youth seemed to generate heat and energy.

But other health concerns were a big issue. A parade of doctors told gruesome stories, complete with color slides, of a variety of exotic diseases. Infant mortality rates, short life expectancy, and overpopulation concerns were drilled home. In ominous tones the doctors admonished, "Take your antimalaria tablets once a week. Never eat raw vegetables unless they have been soaked in potassium permanganate overnight." And then there was the dreaded Mango Fly that laid its eggs in the waistband of clothes hung out to dry. The larva bored under your skin,

15

forming a small pustule. The only way to rid yourself of this infestation is to coat the pustule with petroleum jelly that forces the larva to come to the surface for air where it can be removed with tweezers. "All clothes hung outside must be ironed before wearing." I wondered if anyone in East Africa would be healthy enough to go to school.

Inoculations were administered almost every week; tetanus, polio, typhoid, thypus, and gamma globulin for general immunity and for hepatitis in particular. My personal favorite was typhoid, for within a few hours your arm became red and sore in a three inch square around the point of the injection. It generated enough heat to roast marshmallows. Gamma globulin was given according to weight. One 6'2", 280 lb. male trainee, after receiving the shot, returned to his third floor room at the hotel and fainted. On any given day someone was either feverish, achy, tired, nauseous or weak. But, for fear of being deselected very few trainees missed classes.

To be deselected meant that for some reason (physical, psychological, political) you were found unfit to serve. The criteria for deselection were, I believe, intentionally vague. Outside of being a card-carrying Communists or schizophrenic, we could only imagine what would precipitate deselection.

16

Sometimes lasting six hours a day, language classes dominated the schedule. Swahili is spoken throughout East Africa and, since hundreds of languages are spoken in Kenya and Uganda, it seemed the best choice. Our exact teaching assignments were unknown so it was not possible to learn the local vernacular.

For the first three weeks, no English or textbooks were allowed in language class. Amazingly we quickly learned such useful phrases as "Sina twiga mufukoni mwangu", which means I do not have a giraffe in my pocket. Being young and slightly insane, we would walk down the streets of New York or get on buses and subways and speak to each other in Swahili. One trainee would shout, "Menvu mwako mbichi," pretending to argue when they were really saying, "Your bananas are not ripe." Our instructors were Kenyan, Ugandan and Tanzanian graduate students from various colleges and universities in New York City, who used repetition and pantomime to teach.

Finding your class offered more of a challenge than the class itself. As visitors at Columbia, we used whatever classrooms were available. To further complicate matters, the teachers changed every week so we could hear a variety of accents. Schedules were issued weekly. But you often found the original room assignments changed and your

17

class on the other side of the campus. They also divided us by ability so no one would feel pressured. So, not only did your teacher change, but your classmates changed as well. Mastery of Swahili and/or attendance at language classes was not a requirement, but with the ever-present specter of deselection, absenteeism was low.

The language instructors were the first Africans that many of the trainees had ever met. One of the most fascinating things for me to watch was the interaction of the white female trainees with the language instructors.

Because they were men, in the company of scores of attractive, single women, the instructors flirted furiously. When the women politely but firmly rebuffed their advances, they used the oldest trick in the ethnic book. With an expression somewhere between outrage and hurt they said, "You won't go out with me because I'm black." Often this would do the trick, and the young women would agree to the date.

This was my first experience with "White Guilt." I watched in disbelief as woman after woman was coerced into going out with and tolerating advances from men they didn't really like and who were often not very likeable. Some of the women came to me for advice and I would say, "Tell the man the truth." I tried to explain that going out with someone just to prove you weren't prejudiced is as bad as not going out with someone because you are prejudiced.

I was not exempt. The line used with me was that I was their sister and needed to be schooled in the customs of their country. When I wanted to, I didn't have a problem saying no.

Let me emphasize that not all of the interracial dating was done under duress. Many of the young white women were very willing to date instructors. Many of the trainees didn't know many black people, especially black men. Some relationships became intimate, others just friendships. I remember one particularly naive young lady who was convinced that her newly found love would join her in Kenya and they would be married. He gave her a map to his mother's home which, when she arrived in Nairobi, turned out to be a bar.

Being asked out by the white male trainees was a totally new experience for me. My dating experience was limited. My interracial dating experience was nonexistent. Walking along the street holding hands with a white man made me very uncomfortable. It brought back to me all of things my mother and father told me about white men considering black women as immoral and easy. I recalled

19

how slave masters fathered children by slave women and some of the indignities my mother had experienced growing up in the South. But after a few dates, I soon found that they were just young men who, like me, were searching for something meaningful to do with their lives.

Each trainee had several sessions with a psychiatrist. My therapist, a middle-aged woman, seemed to have more problems than I did or ever would. She talked at length of her struggles with being Jewish and of her ten years of analysis.

With her pencil sharpened and brow furrowed, she said, "I'm very concerned about you. How are you coping being the only black trainee?"

"I'm doing fine. Everyone else seems a bit tense, though," I replied. "They sometimes act as though I blame them personally for racism in America and around the world. Anyway, I'm here to stay, and we'll all just have to deal with it."

Relieving the underlying racial tension became a real issue for me. Being starred at, patronized, or treated with kid gloves got old really fast. I just wanted to finish training, avoid deselection, and go to Uganda. Humor turned out to be the best approach. For example, I teased that there was no way for me to miss language class or a lecture because my absence would be immediately noticed. Or, while they could say that, "One of my best friends is black," I would have to say that, "My only friends are white." Gradually the tension eased.

Chapter 2
Sweetie Pie Does the Big Apple

Besides Nadine, my other two constant companions were Evelyn and Patricia. Evelyn championed the cause of conservation and environmental issues all of her adult life. Her knowledge of flora and fauna amazed me. Real and genuine - - that was Evelyn. No pretension or put on. Evelyn's adventure was life. She looked on the world as a series of wonderful discoveries to be made. Teaching in Uganda provided her with a way to serve and explore.

Evelyn, Nadine and I met Patricia in the cafeteria line at Columbia. We exchanged name, destination and hometown. Patricia was bound for Kenya. When asked where she attended school, Patricia replied, "Galudet College, in Washington, D.C. It's the only college in the United States for the deaf."

The three of us just stood and stared at Patricia. In a brilliant display of deductive reasoning I finally said, "If you're deaf, then you can't hear us." Patricia laughed and replied, "I lip read a little." That was like saying that Barbra Streisand can carry a tune. Patricia's ability to lip read astounded us. From the front, from the side, across the room, she could "hear" everything. Patricia also spoke and lip-read Russian. From that first day she become a part of our group. The four of us, oddly but perfectly matched, went everywhere together.

We explored New York City seeing all of the usual tourist attractions and more. We visited restaurants, theaters and shops, rode subway trains, buses and walked whenever possible. We ate hot dogs, ice cream, popcorn, pizza and pretzels. We rode the Staten Island Ferry at 4:00 a.m., visited Radio City Music Hall, and explored Greenwich Village. We talked, laughed, and cried. We planned, hoped, dreamed, and got into a few sticky situations.

On one occasion near the end of training in December, all the trainees went to the Norwegian Embassy for a holiday party. Norway had volunteers in East Africa and it was a gesture of good will. They served a wonderful hot, spiced wine punch. It was a cold night and we had traveled to the party by subway, so the punch tasted great. We were all feeling pretty mellow after a while and we were exhausted mentally and physically from the rigors of training.

Patricia excused herself, but when she didn't return, we became concerned and went to look for her. She was locked in a stall in the ladies room, fast asleep. This presented a problem. Being deaf, no amount of calling

23

would get Patricia's attention. She was really sound asleep so even hitting on the sides of the stall to make vibrations wouldn't help much. Further, we were guests in a foreign embassy and still could be deselected, so discretion was essential.

While Evelyn acted as lookout, I entered the next stall and crawled under the dividing wall - - luckily about two feet off the ground - - and unlocked the door. Our next problem was to get Patricia out of the bathroom, down a flight of stairs and out of the building. To wake her up, we straightened out her clothes and splashed cold water on her face. We kept telling her to keep her eyes open so she could read our lips, but her level of comprehension was, to say the least impaired.

We got Patricia up and out of the stall. Then with me on one side and Nadine on the other, Evelyn led the way down the stairs both to catch whoever might fall and warn us if anyone was coming. We navigated down the stairs, past the room where the party was and out the door. We pooled our money, hailed a cab, and managed to get Patricia back to the hotel and into bed.

During the night, the three of us took turns watching Patricia so that she would be safe. We were afraid to lock her in her room. She couldn't hear us if we knocked on the door to check on her. She also couldn't hear the phone if we called. The next morning Patricia recovered, and we all had a good laugh about the whole thing.

As a test of the trainees ability to adapt to different cultures and environments, we were sent on a "Live-In". Families in the New York City area were paid to have trainees live with them for three weeks. Mostly black and Latin, many of the families lived in public housing or neighborhoods very different from the hometowns of the trainees. During the three weeks we lived and ate with the families then traveled to Columbia for language classes.

The family I lived with was Puerto Rican, and lived in Spanish Harlem. The household consisted of Carmen, a young woman of twenty-two, her mother, who only spoke Spanish, and her nine-year-old nephew.

As I walked from the subway past the abandoned buildings, the piles of uncollected garbage and the broken streetlights, I pulled my coat tightly around me and took a death grip on my purse and suitcase. I eyed with suspicion every car that passed and everyone I met on the street. As a native Chicagoan, housing projects were not new to me, and although I never lived in one, I had visited them on several occasions. As I arrived at my new home, I noted the sameness of housing projects. There were dozens of buildings, all just alike. There were poorly lit hallways and stairways, unreliable elevators, graffiti. I felt like I was on a sound stage of *West Side Story*, but this was reality.

Carmen and her family put forth a great deal of effort to prepare for my stay. New curtains in the bedroom, a new bedspread and a bedside table and lamp. The small apartment was immaculately clean and quite comfortable.

My three-week stay was uneventful but educational. I walked around the neighborhood with Carmen and visited the community center where she volunteered. I met young people my own age whose upbringing had been very different from mine but whose hopes and dreams were very similar. I learned a great deal but there were two lessons that really benefited me overseas.

First, my host family and others asked why I was there. It was very difficult for me to explain why I was there without insulting my hosts. I couldn't say they were being paid to have me there so I could have "an appropriate cross cultural experience to test my adaptability." I couldn't say I was being sent to live with a poor family in a housing project to see if I could survive. Using all the tact and diplomacy I could muster my standard reply was that since PCVs are sent to far off places and often stationed by themselves, we were being tested on our ability to make friends in a new and unfamiliar environment with people we had never met before.

This experience helped me immensely when, as a PCV, those who considered Peace Corps Volunteers as spies or purveyors of imperialist propaganda questioned my presence in Uganda.

Secondly, I found out how lonely you can be in a room full of people speaking a language you don't understand. Most conversations in the home were in Spanish so I was at a complete loss. I began to feel paranoid and wonder if they were talking about me. They probably weren't, but it was a strange feeling. Once overseas, I became accustomed to hearing a cacophony of tongues and participating in conversations that drifted in and out of several languages. But this first introduction, however brief, made the transition easier.

After our "Live-In", we reconvened at the Paris Hotel. Our experiences affected each one of us differently. We had several group sessions and I saw up close what racism does to white people. For many of the trainees, the "Live-In" was the first time they had been out of their element. Many of them had never been near poor, or black, or Latin people, or any people who didn't think, act and look like they did. To suddenly be thrust into a new

27

environment was too much.

They were incredibly naive. They did not know that people in America lived in the conditions they had seen. For many it was the first time they had been the minority. They stood out in Harlem like I did in the training group.

When you are a minority, you must learn to live in the majority world in order to survive. So I knew how to operate in a white dominated, sometimes hostile world. What to say, what not to say, how to pick up subtle signals of discrimination or danger. They had no such skills and it forced many to dig deep and re-examine themselves and their motives.

Several rethought their decision to go to Africa and left training voluntarily. Others came face to face for the first time with their prejudices. Some refused to admit they had any prejudices and with frozen smiles, insisted that they had been totally unaffected by the experience.

As I listened to my contemporaries, who were like me in so many ways, I realized that on some levels we were light years apart. While racism's effect on minorities had undoubtedly been more direct and devastating, those wealthy, young, white people, totally out of touch with reality had not escaped unharmed. One particular incident sticks in my memory. One of the trainees traveled extensively, and had a charm bracelet with a charm from every country she visited. The bracelet disappeared during her "Live-In".

The matter was discussed in a group setting with a psychiatrist present. Some people blamed the young woman. "Why did you take it with you in the first place? That's really stupid." Others said, "What did you expect, flaunting your wealth like that? You stayed with a poor family. They probably needed the money for food or something. Your insensitivity just proves what a racist you are."

I was livid. "No one had the right to steal, no matter what their circumstances. Excusing such behavior on the basis of ethnicity or economics is insulting and patronizing." Some understood me, some didn't.

After a few more weeks of language classes, and lectures and practice teaching in New York City schools, training was over. Mid-December, 1966, we all went home for the holidays. Only three trainees were deselected; one for being a member of the Communist Party, and two for psychological reasons. As we left New York, there were smiles, tears, hugs, and kisses. We had become a family during the three months of training and saying goodbye, even for a short time, was difficult.

29

My emotions during that Christmas of 1966 bubbled and boiled with a mixture of sadness and expectation. I expected to be homesick and lonely, but the prospect of going to Africa quickened my pulse and fired my imagination.

I filled those few weeks in Chicago with memories: riding the bus downtown, shopping at Marshall Field and Company and Carson Piere Scott, Orchestra Hall, The Art Institute, Michigan Avenue, Saturday matinees, visiting my high school, Buckingham Fountain. My parents hosted a party in my honor and relatives from far and near attended. Advice and good wishes abounded. "You be careful, Sweetie Pie. They have wild animals over there, you know."

"I sure hope no cannibals are in... What's the name of that place you're going again?"

"Bring me back something African."

"Who would have thought it? Little Sara going to Africa; my, my, my."

Then the time arrived. We stood, my parents and I, at another departure gate in O'Hare Airport, just as we had four months earlier, trying to think what to say or what not to say. I didn't see my father cry this time. He just hugged me, held me for a moment, and walked away. My mother and I embraced silently. As I settled into my seat to await take off, I remembered my mother's last words. "After all, two years isn't such a long time, and the experience will be good for you."

Chapter 3

The Garden of Eden

On January 3, 1967, the KLM charter flight took off from New York. For an enthusiastic group of people off on a great adventure, the new Peace Corps Volunteers were surprisingly subdued.

For me, the full import of going to Africa came through. I would be thousands of miles away from home, possibly stationed in a remote area not knowing the local language. What if I got sick? Maybe I should have had my appendix removed as a precautionary measure. Was I really qualified to teach? My students' entire future depended on how well they did on their exams. Was I up to the challenge? But barring the availability of a parachute and outstanding swimming skills, it was a little late to consider going back.

After refueling in Amsterdam and Cairo, the plane turned south over Sudan just as darkness fell. The blackness below was broken by the glow of brush fires. From that height they appeared as dozens of flaming snakes some over 100 miles long slithering across the plains. We were in Africa.

32

The airport in Entebbe, Uganda was deserted when we arrived in the predawn hours of the morning. After leaving sub-zero weather in New York, the blast of eighty-degree heat that greeted us when the door opened was suffocating.

The possibility of becoming self-important was dashed when, before we could deplane, a representative of the Ministry of Agriculture sprayed the cabin with insecticide. We who were inoculated against every disease known to mankind, we who were sacrificing two years of our lives for the good of others were apparently considered bug-carrying foreigners. Our colleagues going to Kenya took off, leaving a somewhat bewildered group standing in the terminal surrounded by baggage and carrying winter coats. Peace Corps staff helped us through customs and a representative of the Ministry of Education gave us a lengthy speech of welcome. Our appreciation for this gesture of good will was mitigated severely by jet lag and fatigue.

The twenty-mile ride from Entebbe to Kampala was our first cross-cultural shock. In Uganda, a former British protectorate, traffic drives on the left. Traveling sixty miles an hour, in the dark, on wrong side of a narrow two-lane road, after seventeen hours in the air certainly gets the

33

adrenaline pumping.

We piled off the bus at the Silver Springs Hotel grateful to still be alive. It was almost 3:00 a.m., but the hotel kept the dining room open to feed us and there another jolt of culture shock awaited us. The tables and waiters were dressed immaculately in white. Each place setting consisted of a dinner plate with two forks on the left, a table knife, a spatula-like fish knife a soup spoon to the right and a spoon and fork placed lengthwise at the top of the plate. Before each course the waiter presented us with a menu card, no less, to see if we wanted soup, fish, entree, desert. My experience with such formal dining was limited but I did know to use the utensils from the outside inward.

The waiters glided through the meal with precision. The food was British and bland by American standards. We who had come to serve Uganda were being served by Ugandans with white napkins over their arms. The strange situation coupled with our exhaustion created a surreal air in the dining room. We finally collapsed in bed about 4 a.m.

As a dutiful Peace Corps Volunteer, I deployed the mosquito net suspended from the ceiling above my bed. The net covered the bed so that I slept in a tent of

34

protection from malaria carrying vermin. However, when I staggered out of my bed towards the bathroom, I forgot about the net and nearly hanged myself. Sure that I was being attacked by some jungle monster, I awakened half the hotel before extricating myself from the net. I was mortified.

The next morning we got money and a final reminder that we were guests in Uganda. Then we set off to explore Kampala on our own. (The unit of currency in Uganda is the shilling. At that time seven shillings was equivalent to $1.00 US)

Technicolor, thy name is Uganda. From the first morning as we rode the bus into Kampala, the brilliant colors overwhelmed me. The green grass, the broad, dark green banana leaves, the stalks of green and yellow bananas hanging from brown stems, the brick red soil, the clear blue sky, the yellow buses some double deckers. The women wore dresses in every color of the rainbow with bold stripes, bright prints and other brilliant intricate designs. Many women wore basutis that are dresses made of seven yards of material wrapped around the body and tied with a decorative sash. Several underskirts are worn giving the wearer a padded, rotund appearance. The men wore business suits, slacks and shirts, shorts or kanzus which are

35

loose fitting, ankle length garments resembling a nightshirts.

The houses were a mixture of single story frame or cement block buildings. Some roofs were shingled others covered with sheets of corrugated tin. A few houses were made of mud and sticks with thatched roofs. There were also large luxurious houses that would be the envy of any American suburbanite. Modern office and bank buildings dotted the horizon as we approached the heart of the city. Several large tourist type hotels had swimming pools and elegantly furnished verandahs where you could enjoy the beautiful weather. The white brick of the Parliament Building sparkled in the sun. There was a huge gold crest hanging above the door, beautifully tended gardens and the red, yellow, and black Uganda flag flying proudly from the roof.

The macadam roads bustled with activity. Cars ranged from well-preserved antiques to sleek late model sports cars. All types of trucks, jeeps, motorcycles and scooters whizzed by. People walked along the sides of the road or rode sturdy, functional bicycles. Most bikes came with a rack over the back wheel where everything from stalks of bananas to car engines could be carried depending on the balance and skill of the one pedaling.

The restaurant food, like the hotel food, had a decidedly British air. But with a little effort we found cafes specializing in traditional Ugandan food, as well as Chinese and Indian fare. Prices were reasonable; hamburger, fries and a soda five shillings ($.70), a good radio 100 shillings ($14.00), a bottle of beer three shillings ($.42). Every shop burst with inventory. If you didn't see what you wanted, just move down the street or around the corner. You could find drug stores, repair shops, furniture, woven mats, baskets and yard goods. The economy pulsed and pounded with vitality.

What surprised us was not the contents of the shops, but the ownership. The majority of the business were owned and operated by Indians and Pakistanis. Africans ran some small shops off the main street and government officials owned a few large commercial establishments, but Asians controlled the economy, wholesale and retail.

From the moment we left the hotel, people shouted greetings and words of welcome in Swahili. "Hamjambo"(How are you?), "Habari gani?" (What news is there?),"Muna walimu?" (Are you teachers?). We tried our language skills and found that we could actually be understood. Most people spoke and understood some English and used Swahili mostly for trading with Asian merchants. It was spoken in a non-grammatical almost pidgin style. There was no evidence of rampant disease and deformities described by the doctors in training. Ugandans gave every appearance of being well fed and healthy.

I found the taxi park fascinating. I would discover that every town had one. They are microcosms of Uganda. In Kampala, the taxi park covered several acres close to the city center. You heard the taxi park before you saw it. Voices shouted out the names of towns "Jinja, Iganga, Mbale, Masaka, Entebbe." Cars for hire abounded to take you almost anywhere in the country. Most were Peugeot 404 station wagons with an additional seat put in the rear storage area so that each car could carry seven passengers and the driver. Throughout the park, vendors hawked everything from roasted peanuts to baby clothes. Barbers cut hair and "shade tree" mechanics improvised repairs for car owners who could not afford "regulation" spare parts.

When you entered the park the blockers descended. Their job was to fill up the taxis. The quicker they filled the taxis the bigger the tip from the driver. Competition was stiff because there were more cars than passengers. Prices were standardized more by general agreement than any kind of government regulation but everyone tried to charge us more because we were "rich" Americans. We had done our homework and insisted on the going rate. We soon became very adept at shopping and travelling in Kampala. It was great fun.

As I wandered through the streets of Kampala during those first days, I realized that I had changed places with the other Peace Corps Volunteer. Now I was a member of the majority and they were the minority. I do not mean to imply that I suddenly gained a new identity, just that I realized the strength of numbers. I recognized the latent potential of a continent of unified black people and the impact they could have.

Uganda was prosperous, beautiful, growing and rich in natural and human resources. It spoke to me in a loud, clear voice saying, "Welcome to the Pearl of Africa."

School assignments were announced about ten days after we arrived. Evelyn went to a school just west and north of Kampala while Nadine was sent to a Catholic girls school located twenty miles east of Kampala. Although the school was classified as a government school, it was still administered by nuns. I was assigned to Nkoma Senior Secondary School near the town of Mbale some 125 miles east of Kampala. No PCV had ever been assigned to this school before.

Departures from the hotel were staggered. Some

traveled to their new homes with headmasters or other
faculty members while others required special
arrangements because of the remote locations of the
schools. A Peace Corps driver and vehicle delivered me to
my destination, dropping off other PCVs along the way.

As we sped east from Kampala to Mbale, the beauty
of Uganda enveloped me anew with its lush green foliage,
the soil alternately brick red or dark rich brown, the thick
almost impenetrable forests, and rolling fields of sugar
cane. There were monkeys chattering in the trees,
countless beautiful birds, monitor lizards basking in the sun
and flowering plants in every color of the rainbow. I tried
to remember the names of the towns and settlements we
passed: Mabira forest, Lugazi, Mbiko, Jinja, Iganga,
Tororo, Bugema, Mbale. I also saw huge charcoal furnaces
where wood slowly burned with very little air to make
charcoal that was used as fuel for cooking. But what did I
really know about Uganda? Relevant chunks of training
lectures began to come back to me.

Uganda is a landlocked republic in East Africa more
than 700 miles from the Indian Ocean. It is bounded on the
north by Sudan, by Kenya on the east, on the south by
Tanzania and Rwanda and on the west by Zaire (now called
the Democratic Republic of the Congo). A portion of its

southern border lies on Lake Victoria, the second largest
lake in the world. From Lake Victoria, near the town of
Jinja, spring the headwaters of the Nile River that flows
4000 miles north to Egypt. Uganda shares the lake with
Kenya and Tanzania.

Slightly smaller than Oregon (91,452-sq. mi.), in
1967 Uganda had population of approximately ten million.
There are three main language groups, Bantu, Nilotic and
Nilo-Hamitic and over fifty languages and dialects are
spoken. English is the official language.

The greater part of the population is concentrated in
a wide band along the shores of Lake Victoria. The Bantu-
speaking people in the south, southwest and southeast
include the Ganda, Soga, Nyoro, Gisu and Nkole. In Bantu
languages, on member of the tribe is a Mu----, multiple
members of the tribe are Ba---, the language is Lu---- and
the area where the tribe lives is Bu----. So the Bagisu live
in Bugisu and speak Lugisu. One member of the Gisu tribe
is a Mugisu. The Nilotic and Nilo-Hamitic tribes live in the
northern half of the country. The structures of these
languages are completely different from the Bantu
languages. The northern area of Uganda was less
developed with medium sized cities and few industries.

Located on both sides of the equator, all areas of

Uganda except the extreme north and east receive abundant rainfall. It rains throughout the year but the wettest months are from March to June. Temperatures are tropical rather than equatorial because Uganda is 3,500 to 5,000 feet above sea level. The rainfall and good temperatures allow crops to be grown throughout the year.

The economy is agriculturally based. The major crops grown for export are coffee, cotton, sugar, tea and tobacco. There is also a copper mine in western Uganda. In 1967 Uganda was methodically expanding its industrial capabilities with factories that processed sugar cane, made matches, cooking oil, soap, hoes, candy, bread, cigarettes, textiles, and beer.

As Peace Corps Volunteers, we were well schooled in the political realities of our presence in Uganda. We had been invited by the government to teach in the secondary schools (high schools). As guests of the Uganda government no association with politics or political activity or even commenting on the politics of the country was allowed.

The President of Uganda, Dr. Milton Obote, was elected Prime Minister in 1962 when Uganda gained independence from Britain. The only political party allowed in Uganda was Obote's Uganda People's Congress

(UPC). He was a member of the Langi tribe from northern Uganda.

We knew that certain groups didn't like Dr. Obote. His fiercest opponents were the Baganda. The Baganda always held a prominent position in Uganda even during colonial times. After independence, Obote defeated a Muganda, Benedicto Kiwanuka in a general election for Prime Minister. In 1963, Edward Mutesa, the Kabaka or tribal king of the Baganda, was elected president of Uganda with Obote as Prime Minister. However, by 1966, Obote had forced the Kabaka into exile in Britain, and assumed the presidency. The Baganda felt betrayed and angry.

There were rumors of large-scale nepotism and corruption in the government and armed forces and we were warned to avoid the army at all costs because of its reputation for brutality. But we saw very few army vehicles on the streets or uniformed soldiers in public places. The Uganda Police dealt with most civil disturbances. Prison guards were also employees of the government. The army, police and prison service were composed mostly of tribes from the north. It was said that the colonial government gave preferences to northerners for military service to make up for the lack of educational opportunities and industrial growth in their area.

43

To me, Milton Obote appeared to be an articulate man who spoke out on issues affecting Uganda in particular and Africa in general. He was a staunch supporter of the Organization of African Unity (OAU) and a strong opponent of the white minority regimes in southern Africa.

Like any other leader, he had enemies and opponents. And, as would be expected, he had ways of finding out who was up to what. We had been warned about Obote's infamous General Service, a group of people from various walks of life who listened out for subversive rumblings and reported them to Obote.

We had to watch what we said and how we behaved. But we didn't feel threatened, intimidated or unsafe. We saw a country of peaceful, law-abiding people ruled by a government that appeared to be making a sincere effort to bring growth and prosperity. We moved about freely and were treated with respect and courtesy wherever we went.

Most people seemed pleased to see us. There were some who resented our presence but this was understandable. After British colonial rule ended, foreign "experts" were regarded by some as unwanted intruders with stereotypical attitudes who took jobs from Ugandans or give unsound advice that could prove detrimental to the country.

When I arrived at Nkoma I found that the school buildings, staff houses and one small dormitory covered an area of several acres. The compound sat on the main road about three miles north of Mbale. I arrived on a Sunday afternoon and found that rather than living in a mud hut with a thatched roof, I had been given a brand new house. The house was locked, unfurnished and without electricity or water. The jeep driver agreed to take me back to town to a hotel when a man came out from the house next door waving and smiling in our direction.

Dan Springs, a British contract teacher, looked like an English schoolmaster. His glasses and somewhat unruly hair reinforced the absent-minded professor image. The headmaster asked Dan and his wife Mary to look after me over the weekend. The Springs three children greeted me shyly, their curiosity evident. I was sure they didn't have many black houseguests, and an American to boot.

Dinner that evening passed pleasantly with the usual exchange of information. For the Springs, like many British contract teachers, Uganda was not their first African experience. Britons in search of adventure and a better life entered service under contract to the British government to use their expertise in "the Colonies". In service, contract personnel lived the good life with spacious houses, servants, a country club, paid home leave, and very ample compensation.

The Springs first assignment was Zambia, formerly know as Northern Rhodesia. When their contract concluded the thought of returning to a Spartan life in a London flat or the English countryside was decidedly unattractive, so they came to Uganda. The Springs introduced me to Mbale and the European community in Uganda.

Mbale, a small, busy town, lies nestled in the foothills of Mount Elgon. Green, lush hillsides are everywhere and rainfall is plentiful. A trademark of many towns in former British colonies is a clock tower and Mbale was no different. The three-mile drive from Nkoma ended at the traffic circle where the clock tower was located. A left exit from the traffic circle accessed the main street.

Shops of all descriptions lined the main thoroughfare: bakeries, butchers, tailors, a post office, coffee shops, banks, restaurants, and bars. There were no supermarkets in Uganda, even in Kampala. Shopping meant visiting all the specialty shops to gather what you needed. Saldana's Grocery stocked the largest variety of items in town and catered to the expatriate community.

Canned food, candy, liquor from the United States and United Kingdom lined the shelves. Fresh vegetables and eggs from local farmers, imported meats, bacon and sausage were also available, but the prices would put quite a strain on a Peace Corps salary. PCVs were paid $100 a month (700 Uganda shillings), enough to live comfortably but economically. I made a mental note to explore the local outdoor produce market on my own.

After visiting several more shops, we went to the Mount Elgon Hotel for tea. Tourism brought millions of dollars to Uganda, so luxurious tourist hotels were built in major cities and run by Uganda Hotels, an agency of the government.

The breathtaking view of the foothills from the lounge of the Mt. Elgon Hotel provided a wonderful backdrop for a meal, drinks, or the uniquely British event of high tea. There were no tea bags here. Real tea leaves were steeped in hot water and the tea strained into a warmed cup. Most people take milk, yes milk, in their tea. (Lemon can be requested.) Tiny tomato, cucumber and egg sandwiches along with cookies and other pastries round out the meal. I enjoyed high tea but visions of greasy hamburgers and milk shakes danced through my head. Gastronomically, it would be a long two years.

I visited the Mbale European Club later that week. This quasi country club had tennis courts, swimming pools, and, on Friday night, fish and chips served wrapped in newspaper, British style. As I sipped my Jim Beam and gingerale, I wondered if I was really in Africa.

Within a week I was settled in my new home and still had a few days before school began. PCVs couldn't own cars. We used public transportation so we could really learn about the people of Uganda. But we did get a bicycle allowance, so I rode my bike into town and explored Mbale on my own. (The students thought it was very amusing for a "rich" American to ride a bike.) My first stop, the open market.

Like the taxi park, you heard the market before you saw it. The sound of hammers pounding metal rose above the voices of the sellers hawking their wares. Upon entering the market the source of the pounding became apparent. A group of craftsmen were transforming metal barrels into charcoal stoves. The barrels are cut into strips to form circles eight to twelve inches in diameter and eight inches in height. Metal legs raise the stoves about six inches off the ground. The inner part is divided into two sections horizontally by a metal grate. The bottom section that has a solid bottom is accessed by a small door.

Charcoal is placed on top of the grate and newspaper or kindling is placed in lower section below the grate. The charcoal ignited by the paper, burns slowly. Pots of food placed on the burning charcoal cook slowly and evenly, staying warm for extended periods of time. These stoves are the prototypes for the popular metal cylindrical charcoal starters.

Every twist and turn of the market brought new wonders. Kiosks selling new and used clothing, dishes, silverware and clothing filled one corner. Sellers covered in black dust hawked gunnysacks and five-gallon cans of charcoal in another area.

Color abounded - - piles of oranges, lemons, limes and pineapples with brown husks and spiny green tops; tomatoes, potatoes of all types, onions, dried beans, fresh beans, peas and peanuts. Exotic smells cascaded through the air. Red, brown and yellow curry and chili powders were mixed to your specifications and used to flavor meat and vegetable dishes. The potency of the mixtures ranged from mild to fiery hot.

Varieties of fresh and dried fish were available as well as sides of beef and goat. The meat hung from hooks and the customer instructed the butcher where to cut. Shopping this way was an adjustment for an American used to plastic wrapped packages in a sanitized display case. The butcher waved away the flies, cut the meat and wrapped it in newspaper or a banana leaf. The quality of the meat varied from day to day and butcher to butcher but the price was reasonable and thorough cooking took care of bacteria. The Asian butcher shop on the main street carried ground beef for hamburgers and spaghetti sauce and on rare occasions, budget allowing, a professional cut of meat.

The only bananas I was familiar came with a picture of Chiquita, but in the open market were varieties of bananas I had never seen. The yellow "Chiquita" bananas were small and very sweet. But most of the bananas were sold green. These many varieties of green bananas are called matoke. Matoke is eaten throughout Uganda but particularly in the southern half of the country. The matoke is peeled with a knife, washed, wrapped in banana leaves and steamed. The hot, steamed bananas are eaten with meat or vegetable sauce. Matoke is sold in stalks or small bunches.

Every day I discovered new shops that fit my budget and tastes. I returned to the country club several times with the Springs and even took lessons in Scottish dancing. Being well rounded is a hard habit to break. When school started, in late January, I was very comfortable in Mbale.

The teaching staff of Nkoma included British contract teachers, Ugandan teachers, Asian teachers and me. The student body of 200 was co-educational. Some of the male students lived in the single dormitory building on the school compound. All other students found their own accommodations in Mbale or surrounding villages.

Although schools were administered by the government,

education in Uganda was not free. From the first grade until college, students paid school fees. The places available were awarded through a series of highly competitive exams. The higher up you go the stiffer the competition and the fewer places available.

After seven years of primary school, students take an examination and only those scoring in the top 10% qualify for places in secondary school. Students are assigned to secondary schools not according to where they live, but by a type of pool system. Principals and headmasters choose the students based on exam grades and the schools the students list as preferences. As would be expected, certain schools are preferred over others. Since schools are not evenly distributed around the country, a student living in western Uganda may be assigned to a school in the northern part of the country.

Many schools have dormitory facilities but others do not so students must find their own accommodations in a strange town and many undesirable situations occur. Some students work as house servants to pay for their rooms or exchange other types of labor for food. Many walk eight and ten miles to school every day.

Despite all these hardships plus the school fees that often exceed the annual family income, places offered in school are rarely refused. Students are very serious about their studies and there is seldom a discipline problem.

During four years of secondary school students take seven to nine subjects all taught in English, which is for most, their third or fourth language. Add to this the complication of being taught by instructors with American, British, Scottish and Indian accents and it is a wonder the students learn anything at all.

At the end of four years of secondary school, the students sit for the East African School Certificate Exam. During three weeks, they take exams on everything they have learned for four years in all subjects.

If they do well, they go on for two years of Higher School, the equivalent of junior college. After two years they take another test and a lucky few are accepted at

Makerere, the only university in Uganda.

University education is paid for entirely by the government. The students who make it that far are truly the smartest, most capable young people in the country. A few teacher-training colleges and technical schools are available but securing a place is very difficult.

Makerere University and Mulago Hospital in Kampala hosted distinguished research fellows on subjects from lymphoma to the diet of fish in Lake Victoria. Graduates of Makerere formed the educated elite of East Africa and held important positions all over the world.

Since the School Certificate Exam determined their future, the students only wanted to be taught material in the syllabus on which the exam is based. Syllabi for all School Certificate subjects were readily available and the students would follow along as you taught and check off each topic. Any deviation from or addition to the syllabus would be questioned. This made what to teach a relatively simple choice but drastically affected how the material was taught.

Students demanded notes, pages and pages of notes. They wanted the teacher to dictate notes and pass out sample questions and answers to be memorized. Imagine learning and retaining so much in a foreign language. Some of the topics covered, I learned in college.

53

The students were delightful, polite and totally serious about schoolwork. I learned so much more from them than they did from me. One of my most memorable experiences occurred on my first day in the classroom.

Determined to make a good impression, I prepared a lecture on a subject I knew well: the structure and function of the human kidney. The day before, I drew a diagram of a kidney cross section on the board with colored chalk. I put definitions of all the most important terms on the board as well. I even rehearsed my lecture several times to an empty classroom.

When I arrived in class the next morning, all of the students stood up as I entered. It took me totally by surprise even though I had been told that this was done as a sign of respect for the teacher. I took my place at the front of the room and they remained standing. Finally, I figured out they were waiting for permission to be seated. As I began the lecture, my voice shook a little at first, but grew stronger as I continued. Every student dutifully took notes, and copied the diagram. This teaching thing was a snap.

When I finished, I asked for questions. One student shyly raised his hand, stood and said, "What is a kidney, Madam?" I was dumbfounded. They had not understood one word I said but were too polite to interrupt. When I probed further, I found that I spoke to rapidly and slurred my words together like "wader" instead of "WA-ter". It was a very humbling and enlightening experience. That taught me to always check with my class to make sure I was being clear.

Life as a Peace Corps teacher was challenging. I spent a great deal of time preparing lessons and trying to balance the students need for pages of notes with my own need to be creative. One way I got to know the students was through my Peace Corps book locker. The Peace Corps provided each volunteer with a book locker containing authors as diverse as Kurt Vonnegut and Ayn Rand. The students would come and borrow the books and would often ask me questions about what they had read. This led to many lively and interesting discussions about everything from marriage to world politics. The books were always treated with great care and returned promptly.

I also had to learn "British" English. Cookies are biscuits, biscuits are scones, the trunk of the car is the boot, the hood of the car is the bonnet, an elevator is a lift, sausages and potatoes are bangers and mash, and a wrench is a spanner. In addition, the students had their own problems with English.

For instance, in some Bantu languages the letters l

and r are interchangeable depending on what they precede or follow. The students tried to apply the same rules to English with amusing results like these:

"When the President finished speaking everyone started crapping (clapping)."

"My father works on the Lailload (railroad).

"Women should be educated so that they will know what to do during an national erection (election)."

After reading a Newsweek magazine, one student asked why the United States was sending animals to Viet Nam. I was really puzzled until he showed me the article about the "gorilla" (guerilla) fighters.

On one of my most memorable weekends I visited the home of a student. We took a bus from Mbale into the foothills of Mount Elgon and then began to climb. The student assured me that it was only a short walk up the path to his house. The word "short' evidently lost meaning in translation. We walked and climbed for well over an hour and finally, near sunset, reached his home.

As is Ugandan tradition, I was royally treated. His parents and other relatives greeted me warmly. Food and good will abounded throughout the evening. Late that night when I found myself with a few moments alone, I stood outside in the crisp air and looked up at the clear night sky.

The stars and moon shone brilliantly almost close enough to touch. I recognized some of constellations and they seemed more real to me than ever before. It was one of the most peaceful and beautiful scenes I ever experienced.

The Peace Corps kept tabs on us, especially health wise. Every month we completed a questionnaire for the Peace Corps doctor about health problems. About twice year the doctor would come to visit and check us personally. I had a slight case of dysentery once and a few chiggers in my toes but was otherwise quite fit.

During school vacations, the Peace Corps held a big meeting of all the volunteers and we would exchange experiences and get reacquainted. On the Fourth of July, the American Embassy held a picnic complete with hot dogs, hamburgers and ice cream. There were also Americans in Uganda working with USAID and even a few missionaries who would open up their homes to PCVs on holidays

The rainy season fascinated me. You could set your watch by the rain. It rained at exactly 2 p.m. every day at Nkoma. First in big heavy drops and then in torrents so heavy you couldn't see more than a few inches in front of you. The driveway in front of my house turned into a river of red mud. It rained for about an hour and then just as quickly, stopped. Within a few moments the sun would be shining again.

Up on the slopes of the foothills of Mount Elgon, the rain could be soft and warm and gentle, almost a mist. The rich dark volcanic soil slowly soaked in moisture and produced some of the finest coffee in the world.

As I came to know more about Uganda, I was struck by the way aid from abroad, no matter how well intentioned, was often ill conceived. For instance, John Deere tractors were given to Uganda to assist in farming and other activities. The problem was that the spare parts for the tractors were very expensive and had to be sent from thousands of miles away.

One more example: The United States Agency for International Development (USAID) was instrumental in building a secondary school for girls in Tororo. It was a beautiful school but the way it was equipped was questionable. In the home economics department there were American style gas ranges and refrigerators. While using these appliances must have been a learning experience for the students, it had little connection to the reality of their lives. Also, the sockets for the light bulbs at the school had threads for screw-in bulbs like in the US. Light fixtures in Uganda were made to accommodate the two-pronged light bulbs that twisted into the socket. Light bulbs for the school had to be imported from West Germany.

During school vacations and on weekends I traveled; sometimes alone, sometimes with other Peace Corps people. I visited Evelyn and Nadine or went on sightseeing excursions. On these trips I often used taxis. Since the school was on the main road, I could easily get a taxi to Mbale, for 2 shs. ($.28). In Mbale at the taxi park there were cars going everywhere. Usually three or four cars would be competing for passengers. Sometimes the drivers would squeeze in one or two extra people but on long journeys they seldom overloaded because the Uganda Police were strict about carrying excess passengers.

The fare from Mbale to Jinja was 10 shs. ($1.40) for a journey of eighty miles, then 5 shs. ($.70) from Jinja to Kampala, a distance of fifty miles. The drivers were a little reckless but you eventually got used to it. Taxis ran from early morning until 9 or 10 p.m. You seldom had to wait. A round trip from Mbale to Kampala could easily be done in half a day. Of all my trips, there are two that stand out in my memory.

The first was to Kidepo and Murchison Falls National Parks. Evelyn, her housemate Connie, a PCV, and two young American men visiting Uganda completed the group. Thousands of tourists came to Uganda to see wildlife in their natural habitat and Murchison Falls National Park on the banks of the Nile, had the worlds most abundant crocodile and hippo populations.

Beautiful, modern tourist lodges provided accommodation in the parks and poachers were severely punished. Elephants, water buffalo, antelope, giraffe, rhinoceros and birds of all descriptions flourished. Tourism was a major source of income for Uganda.

We drove north towards Kidepo National Park. Fifty miles or so north of Mbale, near the town of Soroti in Teso district, the country becomes very sparsely populated. We drove for miles and saw only a few scattered houses and the roads became rougher and narrower. We finally reached Moroto, the largest city in Karamoja district. The tribe who lives in that area is the Karamajong. The men wear no clothes, only occasionally a cape, and headpieces made of hair and red clay. The women dresses in cow hides and decorate themselves with necklaces and other ornaments made from chrome or any other kind of metal they can find.

The Karamajong are nomadic cattle herders who travel great distances looking for grazing areas for their herds. At certain time of the years, they stop, plant crops and build temporary houses. Karamajong are often involved in violent disputes with neighboring tribes over stolen cattle. Karamoja is not the place to be stranded. As we drove, we met very few cars but we did see several groups of Karamajong who waved and were even kind enough to pose for pictures with us. We were confident we could reach Kidepo before dark.

But when we came around a bend in the road, suddenly we had a problem. A rainstorm had wiped out about a fifty-foot wide stretch of the road. Beyond that, the road was fine. What to do? Turn around and go back? No. We were young, determined and insane. We would get through.

We filled the damaged part of the road with rocks and dirt. The Volvo we drove had good tires and we were sure we could make it. By the time we finished our road repairs, quite an audience of Karamajong had gathered. We couldn't understand what was being said but obviously they thought we were not very bright. If the car got stuck and had to be left, it would be stripped of every inch of chrome and all the tires. Not to mention the danger we would face walking back to the nearest town.

Finally everything was ready. We all walked

cautiously across the damaged section except the young man who was the designated stunt driver. Maneuvering carefully but with sufficient speed not to get stuck, he successfully crossed the bad patch. A cheer went up from the Karamajong and a sigh of relief from us. We continued our trip and reached Kidepo at dusk.

The next day we hired a Land Rover and driver and spent all day watching animals. We stopped not six feet from an elephant with huge tusks. Families of warthogs scurried through the tall grass, their tails straight up in the air. The eerie laugh of hyenas could be heard as they feasted on the remains of a lion kill. A black rhino charged us and only stopped because the driver turned off the engine. Rhinos do not see well but they have very keen hearing. When the engine stopped he did not know where we were and soon went off in the opposite direction. We spent the evening next to a roaring fire watching the sun set over the vast savannah.

Next we moved westward to Murchison Falls. The two lodges there provided wonderful food and excellent accommodations and were filled to capacity with tourists. We took a launch trip along the Nile to the base of the thunderous falls. Hundreds of crocodiles and hippos lined the banks and played around the boat. The hippos swam under the boat and rocked it slightly, letting us know they could capsize us if they wanted to. Then they surfaced, opened their huge mouths to pose for pictures. Crocodiles slithered off the banks and swam along side the boat perhaps hoping for someone to fall overboard. These beasts are really gray rather than green and can easily be mistaken for logs.

Being on a limited budget, we could not stay in the lodge. No one was allowed to camp outside because of the elephants and buffalo that would come right up to the lodge at night so we rented a cabin with campbeds and mattresses. Sleeping bags were standard Peace Corps equipment. Wooden shutters covered the windows and we left them open as we slept. About midnight, Connie awoke to a shuffling, grunting noise. More than a little nervous about being so close to nature, she let out a blood curdling scream, leapt to her feet and shouted "There's a warthog in the window!" That woke up everyone. We looked around outside but couldn't see anything. We finally calmed Connie down and went back to sleep. The next morning the park ranger identified the hoof prints out side the cabin not as warthog tracks but hippo tracks. That was a little too close to the "Wild Kingdom".

The other trip was to the Serengeti National Park in

Tanzania. Nadine, Evelyn, Connie and I rented a car and drove east to Kenya, picked up Patricia and then headed south to Tanzania. We reached the Serengeti Plains during the great migration when the grazing animals move south searching for water.

No matter how much you have read or think you know, nothing quite prepares you for what you see. And if you are young and inexperienced in life, it can almost be beyond comprehension. So as my four fellow Peace Corps Volunteers and I drove down the unpaved but well maintained road in Tanzania that day and topped the hill, we gasped audibly at the sight.

At first you think the ground is covered with odd shades of vegetation rippling in the breeze, but on closer examination you see that the movement is the apparently random motion of thousands of animals. The vast plains of the Serengeti National Park were covered with zebra, antelope, gazelle and wildebeests. Some stood still watching us with bored familiarity rather than curiosity or fear. Others grazed and flicked away flies with their tails.

The young wildebeests (gnus) pawed the ground and, with lowered heads, challenged their rivals by bellowing loudly and darting in and out of the herd. Mothers of all breeds hovered over their calves, licking and nuzzling while being ever vigilant for predators. Birds fluttered and hopped from one animal to the other eating insects from their coats and dropping to the ground to scrounge for seeds. Scores of zebra moved in and out of the surrounding brush. Their unmistakable coloring transformed magical into camouflage as the sun filtered down through the trees and brush. They moved with an odd prancing gait and tossed their heads from side to side emitting a nasal whinny.

Suddenly, as if by some silent signal, the entire herd swung about and moved off to the left or right raising clouds of dust. As the herd moved, scores of animals crossed the road in front and in back of our small car, shaking the ground but never once hitting each other or us. It was as if they were guided by natural radar telling them which way to turn.

Every year, nature mysteriously signals this herd of many species to turn as one to the south and follow the water, and the Great Migration begins. This undulating river of life flows across the arid African plains living, dying, birthing, fighting, and surviving.

The next day we played tourist on a mini-bus with a guide and a group of German tourists. We stopped ten feet from a pride of lions, saw a leopard sprawled on a tree branch and laughed at prairie dogs chasing each other in and out of their burrows.

As we left the park two days later, a cheetah came down from the rocks and loped along side the car. We steadily increased our speed but the cat kept pace effortlessly. Even at 60 mph the cheetah stayed with us. It was the perfect running machine; sleek, powerful, and perfectly tuned. Finally, the cheetah decided we were slowing him down and turned on the after burners. Although our speedometer said seventy the cheetah accelerated, cut across the road in front of us and disappeared into the bush.

We continued to the town of Moshi in Tanzania at the foot of Mt. Kilmanjaro. As we approached we got our first glimpse of Kilimanjaro. It stood isolated, as if put there by mistake. Its snow covered cap in surreal contrast to the equatorial heat below. The hotel arranged for guides and porters and the day after we arrived we began to climb the mountain. It really wasn't a climb it was more of a long uphill walk. The porters ran past us carrying baggage and boxes of provisions, while we struggled to carry our own body weight and a camera. As we passed through villages, the people shouted greetings and words of encouragement in Swahili. We waved, smiled and struggled to breathe in the increasingly rarified air.

As we climbed, soil and rock changed from the familiar red East African dirt to volcanic gray rock and dark soil. The snow-capped peak appeared and disappeared from view as we made our way to the top and flowers of every color dotted the hillside. I particularly remember a meadow covered with knee high yellow and lavender flowers. The air was crisp and cool and the sun shone brightly.

We slept in our clothes and under blankets to ward off the very cold nights but during the day we worked up a sweat with the steady uphill climb. Tired and stiff, we reached the hut at the base of the summit on the third day. At 4 a.m. the next morning we would begin our climb so that we could see the sun rise from the top of the mountain.

Everyone was experiencing some degree of nausea, headache or fatigue due to the altitude. An hour after arrival at the hut, Evelyn, who was the most experienced hiker and climber among us, suddenly developed trouble breathing. She actually turned blue. We all panicked. "Put her feet up!" "Elevate her head!" "Give her mouth to mouth !" And all Evelyn could say was, "I have to go to the bathroom." The guides insisted that she go down to a lower elevation immediately. Nadine and I were in better shape than anyone else was, so after walking up eleven miles that day, we turned around and walked back down eleven miles the same evening. We never made it to the top.

Evelyn recovered quickly and we took our time going back down to the hotel where the only things we wanted were a hot bath and a bed. I have never been so tired in my life. However, the hot bath was not a great idea. While it felt good and was relaxing, all the unused muscles we abused on the climb had been too cold to hurt until we warmed them up. I dropped a spoon at dinner that night and everyone was too stiff and sore to pick it up. It took us about two days to walk properly again.

During these trips we moved freely, crossing borders with no problem. Our baggage was seldom checked and if so, very superficially. We crossed paths with tourists from Britain, France, Germany, Holland, Australia, Scandinavia and the United States, some on their second or third trip to East Africa. We marveled at the natural, unspoiled beauty of East Africa.

When Winston Churchill first saw Uganda, he called it the Garden of Eden. Whatever one's beliefs on Creation, there could be no more perfect place for life to begin than here on these vast plains, in these fertile valleys, soaked by abundant rain, and warmed by perpetual sunshine.

Chapter 4
Mukholi's Grandson

After being at Nkoma for six months, I was joined by another Peace Corps Volunteer, Rachel. She had trained to go to Tanzania, but things changed and she was in Uganda teaching English. Being new girls in town, we drew some attention. Young men in the area often drove out to Nkoma and asked us out for dinner or a drink. We exercised caution in accepting invitations, but we did go out regularly.

Social life in Uganda was pleasant and varied with a variety of movies, bars, restaurants, and nightclubs. All types of alcoholic beverages were available, the most popular being beer and a Uganda made gin called Waragi. The bottles of beer were large and we learned to drink slowly because as soon as you finished one bottle, another one appeared. Every man at the table bought a round of drinks. Any man who sponged was a social outcast. As invited guests, Rachel and I didn't buy drinks. Ugandan society was chauvinistic, but women were highly respected. A man could drink to excess and even be unfaithful without censure, but if he didn't provide the necessities of life for his wife and family his fellows took him to task.

The Mt. Elgon Hotel or the Bugisu Coffee Union
(BCU) hall served as sites for dances in Mbale. (The BCU
bought the coffee crop from local farmers and then sold it
to the government for export.) The live music was an
eclectic mixture. Ugandans love country western music.
Jim Reeves songs played on the radio and were performed
at every dance. The other popular music came from Zaire,
sung in the Zairian language of Lingala. The rhythm and
pulse of the music captivated you. It pulsed, breathed and
flowed with the simple, fluid movements of the dance.

One evening in July, Rachel and I double dated with
Peter Wanambwa and his brother James who had recently
returned from Canada. James spouted all of the latest
American slang and demonstrated all the latest dance steps.
I considered him a shallow, pretentious, showoff. Standing
several inches over six feet, lankly, and lean best described
James. Big brown eyes, small moustache, and a mellow
voice completed the picture. He looked a lot like Harry
Belafonte. Charm, the man oozed charm, so I went out with
him again, and again. That shallow, phony first impression
melted away to reveal a friendly, open man with a very
serious side. James, a Mugisu, was the oldest son in a
family of nine. His father William Stanley Wanambwa, one
of the country's most experienced and respected civil

servants, graduated from Makerere University and served as District Commissioner in several areas of the country. That position is the equivalent of being governor of a state.

James returned from Canada before finishing his studies because his father was ill. As the eldest son, responsibility for the younger children, his mother, and family affairs passed to James on the death of his father.

Growing up in Mbale, James accumulated many friends and acquaintances. Whenever we went out, he met someone he knew. I met James' sister Frances, her husband Michael and their children on a weekend trip to Kampala. They greeted me warmly and seemed a bit surprised that James brought me to visit. Michael worked at Makerere University. Frances worked for the government. Patrick, another brother, worked for the Jinja Municipal Council and often traveled to Mbale to visit. To my surprise, one of my students at Nkoma was also James' brother. (Not all members of a family use the same surname.)

Our relationship reached a new level when James took me to meet his mother. She divided her time between Jinja with her husband, and the family home in a village called Butta, a few miles outside of Mbale where we went to see her. James' oldest sister Eileen would be there also.

James and I said very little as we drove. My palms

sweated, my mind raced. What would I say? Was I
dressed properly? Did this introduction have some deeper
meaning? This was another fine cross-cultural mess, I'd
gotten myself into.

What did I know about Janet Wanambwa? James
described her as the backbone of the family. She was a
woman who managed her large family in addition to the
family farming enterprises. Devoutly religious, her love of
God was matched only by her concern for others.

We turned off the dirt road and bounced down a
long rutted driveway. Two women sat on a colorful
women mat on the front porch. Shade trees dotted the yard
and there was a small family cemetery plot to the left of the
driveway. The glass windowpanes, tin roof and ample size
of this cement blockhouse showed the high status of the
family.

The bright colors in the basutis James' mother and
sister, Eileen, wore sparkled in the afternoon sun. We
exchanged pleasantries as we shared tea. Then Janet
Wanambwa made a startling statement that Eileen
translated: "In our culture, when a young man brings a
woman to meet his mother, it means that he is planning to
propose". A hint of a smile touched her eyes and pulled up
the corners of her mouth.

I didn't know how to respond so I mumbled something brilliant and original about it being James' decision and crossing bridges when we got to them. She laughed. I laughed. Eileen laughed. Everyone laughed but James. He just stared at me with big brown eyes and an unreadable expression. My heart sank and sprouted wings at the same time. I was in deep trouble.

A few days later, James dropped by unexpectedly. He asked me to go for a ride and we drove around aimlessly for a while making small talk before heading back to Nkoma. As I reached for the door handle, James placed his hand over mine. He looked into my eyes and said "I've been trying to build up the nerve for this all afternoon." The world stopped turning. James took a deep breath and said "Will you marry me?" Silence. I imagined this moment in my mind thousands of times but now the moment had arrived, I couldn't speak. "Give me a few days to think, James," I whispered as I flung open the door and bolted like a frightened fawn.

I loved James. His sisters and brothers Patrick, Peter, Paul, Michael, Connie, Margaret, Frances and Eileen were the siblings I missed being an only child. They treated me with kindness and patience and never made me feel like an outsider. But marrying James presented numerous complications. It meant only seeing my parents every few years, living in an unfamiliar culture, and never seeing I Love Lucy re-runs again. It also meant resigning from the Peace Corps. But I loved James and his family. Wasn't this the ultimate adventure? I would move from life as a Peace Corps Volunteer, to an exotic wedding, to a life of daring escapades in Africa. How could I refuse?

James was happy and terrified when I accepted and that made two of us. Being a brave but not foolhardy soul, I wrote rather than called my parents about the impending nuptials. My mother sent a list of questions and a "request" that James write and confirm his intention to marry me. Control, thy name is Sara Jones McWright. The next hurdle to clear was meeting James' father. He still lived in the District Commissioner's house in Jinja although his illness prevented him from working. Tall and lanky like his sons, William Stanley Wanambwa greeted me warmly. No one told me what was wrong, but cancer seemed a pretty safe bet. Weak, wan, but still a commanding presence, he explained my role as James' wife.

"My father, Mukholi was a chief among the Bagisu. He married thirty wives and fathered over 200 children. Many of the people in and around Butta are our relatives." Well, I thought, as long as they all didn't come to dinner at

75

the same time and I didn't have to remember all their names, I should be all right.

He continued, "Of all of his sons, Mukholi chose me to succeed him as head of the family. James' being my first son becomes head of the family when I die. As his wife you must be prepared to share the responsibilities he will face."

"What responsibilities, sir?" I asked, my voice trembling slightly.

"Four of my children are still in school. You must help with their school fees if needed. James will spend a lot of time helping his mother at Butta. On occasion, family members will call on James to settle disputes usually over land and money. Great demands will be made on his time. You must be strong, patient and understanding. Do you think you can do that?" I swallowed hard and then mustering as much conviction in my voice as possible said, "I will do the best I can, sir."

My parents came from Chicago for the wedding on what was surely an incredible adventure of them both. As far as I know, this was the first time either of them had flown. My father nearly backed out but my mother, as usual, took charge and told him that if he could go or stay but if he didn't go she would make him pay for it for the rest of his life. They bought two tickets the next day. My mother would finally get to Africa, not as a missionary, but as mother of the bride. My father, who never expressed any ambition to go anywhere, would have travel and adventure thrust upon him.

They were both overwhelmed by Uganda. Their knowledge of Africa was movies and TV news: Tarzan, disease, famine, war, cannibals and bare breasted women. Instead they found beautiful buildings, cultured, friendly people, beautiful scenery and all the comforts of home.

My parent's stayed in the District Commissioner's house and were very impressed by its size and elegance. However, at the first meal, my mother raised her glass of water and paused before she drank. I looked over at her and, using an ancient form of communication only known to parents, she gave an imperceptible tilt of the head and flick of the eye to silently ask if the water was safe to drink. I returned her nod indicating that she could drink and have no fear of intestinal distress. After the wedding they toured the country. They took thousands of pictures at the game parks. My father said "Your mother took a picture of every blade of grass in Uganda from both sides."

We were to be married in Mbale by the Rev. John Wasikye, a long time family friend. Several weeks before the wedding, he met with us for counseling. He stressed the enormity of the step I was taking. Did I really want to live so far from my family? Could I adjust to life in an unfamiliar culture? Did James understand that having a foreign wife presented challenges? He gave us both a great deal to think about. We talked of hours about all of the possible difficulties we would face, but we were convinced that we belonged together. James was confident of being successful with his dairy farm so that we could make trips to the United States regularly. We even talked about sending our children to America for college.

My wedding day, April 20, 1968 dawned sunny and clear.
From the outside, Mbale Cathedral appears to be a dark and somber place but once inside you find a breathtaking church full of light and space. The rows of benches are spacious and inviting. The aisles are wide and the altar open and uncluttered so that everyone can watch the ceremony.

Nadine, Evelyn, Connie, Patricia and James' two younger sisters Margaret and Connie served as bridesmaids. Rachel was maid of honor. They wore blue satin like short dresses and I wore a simple long white dress of the same material. We flew in the face of British tradition when James and his best man wore white tuxedo jackets instead of morning coats. My father gave me away. It was the only time I ever saw my Dad in a tuxedo.

Aunts, uncles, cousins, friends filled the sanctuary and spilled over outside. I was so nervous my legs shook as I walked down the aisle. Both our voices and hands trembled as we exchanged vows and rings and after what seemed like hours, the deed was done. I was Mrs. James Henry Kabole Wanambwa.

We rode to the reception in a red Mercedes rather than a black car as was tradition. The reception rocked with dancers and drummers and there was liquid cheer and food in abundance. After the reception, the wedding party traveled to Butta to celebrate with those who didn't come to the ceremony. Later that night, a party was given in our honor in Mbale. It was an unforgettable day. The next day, we left for our honeymoon in the Kenyan coastal town of Mombassa.

The first two years of our marriage brought great sorrow as well as great joy. On our way home from the honeymoon, we had an auto accident. James broke his thigh and several ribs and badly scraped his right arm. I was unhurt. He spent the first four months of our marriage in Jinja hospital, in traction - - how romantic. We lived in

79

Jinja within walking distance of the hospital. The first two months, I slept in the hospital room with James because he was unable to feed himself. I would teach all day, go home and rest a while, then return to the hospital at dinnertime.

All delusions of romance and perfection were quickly dispelled. James and I saw each other sick, tired, grumpy and frustrated. He felt like a failure because he couldn't take care of me and I felt over burdened because I had to take care of his every need. But our marriage held together and we leaned on each other for support.

I secured a teaching position at the Pravatiben Muljibahai Madhvani Girls School. A very different experience from Nkoma because most all of the students were girls, most were Asian, and some very wealthy. The school was named for the Madhvani family, who contributed a lot to Uganda. Just outside of Jinja the Madhvanis built an industrial complex know as Kakira. There was a sugar plantation and refinery, a candy factory, a cooking oil factory, a soap factory and the sumptuous homes of the Madhvani family. The factories employed thousands of people.

The quality of the medical care at the government run hospital was excellent. Those who could pay had private or semi-private rooms. Those who were unable to pay were cared for in wards, but no one was turned away. By September 1968, James had progressed from traction, to a cast, to crutches. But the joy of his recovery dimmed when we received word that his father was near death. Just before the wedding my father-in-law went to England for cancer treatment and we were told that he would improve slightly and then deteriorate. During the months that James was hospitalized, he became more and more frail. James rushed to his father's side and was with him when he died. The body was taken to the house in Butta.

My brother-in-law Patrick and I arrived at Butta, in a torrential downpour. The body lay in the front room surrounded by mourners, wailing and moaning. The women keened. Keening is a high pitched sound somewhere between a yodel and a whistle. The mourners pulled me towards the body and I really didn't know what to do. My mother-in-law intervened, took my hand, and led me to the back bedroom and instructed me to stay there.

For the next three days, I watched with fascination as a stream of mourners came and went. Some rolled on the ground crying and moaning, some sang hymns, some sat quietly or spoke consoling words to the family. All of the immediate family members wore an article of the deceased clothing around their waists. Before dawn on the morning

81

of the funeral, the widow was taken to the river for a special ceremony, the details of which I never learned. James' injury limited his ability to participate but a group of elders took him outside, removed his shirt and doused him with cold water. I never fully understood the significance of it all and I felt very foreign and out of place.

On the second afternoon, James' informed me that special visitors were expected and that I must be ready to greet them. Dressed in a basuti a few sizes too large, I joined the other female family members on mats on the floor in the front room. A stream of mourners flowed by, some in suits, some barefoot and in tattered shorts and shirts. Then he arrived wearing a khaki uniform and a dark green flight cap. He was so tall he had to bend over to enter the house. From my vantagepoint on the floor he seemed to be eight feet tall. His wide body filled the doorway, blocking out the light. His skin was so black that is almost seemed bluish purple.

"Who is that?" I whispered to my sister-in-law Eileen.

"That Major General Amin, the head of the army. He's here to represent President Obote," she replied.

Amin turned his penetrating gaze on me as he circled the room greeting the family. This man exuded

82

power and force. A sense of relief washed over me as he
moved on. His wife Kay Adroa Amin accompanied him.
A beautiful soft spoken woman, she grasped my hand and
smiled warmly as she expressed her condolences. They
certainly seemed and odd match.

The funeral was held in Mbale Cathedral where a
few months before, we celebrated our wedding. Rev.
Wasikye presided. As the procession returned to Butta,
people were standing three deep on the side of the road
starting a mile from the house and all the way up the
driveway. When the cortege came into view, a great wave
of wailing and keening arose. The eerie, moving sound
chilled me and made me cry. Standing around the open
grave, the crowd pushed in on us and I feared we would fall
into the open pit. The final prayers could hardly be heard
over the noise of the crowd. It was an outpouring of
sadness, and tribute for a much beloved man and leader.

Tradition dictated a celebration of the life of the
deceased three days after the burial. The preparation for the
feast began early in the morning. I was not asked to help. I
think because I am American it was assumed that I needed
at least a double oven gas range and food processor to
prepare even a simple meal. I took no offense at being
excluded, it gave me time to rest and regroup after the

strain of the funeral.

Earlier I heard the bleating of the goats and lowing of the steer being slaughtered in a field far behind the house. After dressing and butchering the meat was divided into piles. The tender pieces were roasted over charcoal fires, the less choice sections placed in a variety of pots to make savory stews and soups. Onions, curry powder, bamboo shoots, peanut sauce, tomatoes and other powders and seeds I didn't recognize blended together filling the air with exotic smells. Twenty or so chickens were plucked and prepared to be roasted or stewed.

The women, in their colorful dresses, bustled around the yard laughing and shouting instructions. The young children fetched and carried water, pots, pans, whatever was needed. Mounds of green matoke bananas, were peeled, wrapped in banana leaves and steamed over an open fire along with sweet potatoes, yams, and cassava root. Dried beans and peas, soaked over night, simmered in covered pots.

Just after noon, everything was ready. Members of the deceased's family were served, while the guests helped themselves. I assumed my sitting position on a mat on the porch. First soap and pans of water were brought to wash the hands. The steaming mashed bananas were placed on a plate with sweet potatoes and pieces of roasted goat and beef. The soups and meat stews were served in individual brightly colored metal bowls. The art of eating was to shape the bananas into a flat mass, make an indentation with the thumb and scoop the stew or soup into the mouth. Sweet potatoes are broken into large pieces and dipped in the sauce. The ritual of eating is leisurely, with bowls refilled many times. Hands moved from plate to bowl to mouth with rhythm and ease.

My favorite was the peanut sauce. Peanuts were pounded into a smooth paste, mixed with water and curry powder to make a creamy sauce. The sharpness of the curry interacted deliciously with the sugary sweetness of the potatoes and the tangy bite of the bananas. Bamboo shoots were mixed with some of the peanut sauce to add an extra crunchiness. The chicken, cooked to tender perfection, fell off the bone. The roasted meat lightly seasoned with red pepper brought tears to the eyes and fire to the tongue. The toughest cuts of meat melted in the mouth after hours of slow cooking and dried beans and peas became soft and succulent.

When the body finally demanded a stop to what the taste buds said must continue, the soap and water were brought again for hand washing. Everyone then sat back satisfied that they had paid due tribute to the departed soul and that he has somehow feasted with them.

Several months after the funeral, James and I returned to Butta for our installation as leaders of the family. All the elders of the family gathered. We sat on ancient ceremonial stools with exquisite black and white Colobus monkey skins draped around our shoulders while the elders of the family explained our duties. Though my understanding of Lugisu was limited, I understood enough. James was responsible for taking care of his mother and siblings as well as acting a mediator in any matters that were brought to him by other family members. I was to support him, mother his children and act as hostess to all relatives who might visit us in Jinja.

I must admit that sometimes I resented the amount of time and money that we had to give to the family. Several of James' siblings were still in school and needed fees for school. We might just be squeaking by financially but if unexpected visitors came to visit from the village, we had to go and buy special treats for them. I understood the tradition and agreed to it but it I really had to bite my tongue on several occasions.

After the funeral, our lives were very ordinary. I taught school and James worked to build his dairy farm. He would occasionally go the Butta to help his mother and take care of family business. As the new leader of the family his presence was required for major decisions or to settle disputes.

The only real excitement I can recall occurred one evening in December, 1969 when James and I were I Kampala and I was several months pregnant with our first child. We were on our way back to our cousin's house about 10 p.m. and we noticed cars driving very erratically and several military vehicles speeding through town.

About 3 a.m. our cousin called from the hospital to say he had been beaten up the army at a roadblock. An attempt had been made on President Obote's life and the army was out in force looking for the conspirators. A number of people were killed that night but by the next day the army was no longer in evidence and things got back to normal. President Obote was slightly injured, but recovered. The next month Brigadier Okoya, a senior army officer and his wife were murdered at their home. One of those rumored to be involved in the Obote assassination attempt and the Okoya murders was Major General Amin.

May 10, 1970 our son Edward Stanley Mukholi Wanambwa was born. I had an uneventful pregnancy and a normal deliver. Again, I found the care and service in the hospital excellent.

I delighted in motherhood. Edward presented new challenges every day. He was a boisterous, active child who did not want to sleep because he might miss something. Domestic labor was inexpensive, so we hired an ayah (nanny) to take care of the baby and a young man to clean our small house and do some of the cooking.

To supplement our income, James worked with Uganda Television as part of the team that covered the visit of Pope John Paul VI to Uganda. This being the first visit of a reigning Pope to Africa in hundreds of years, elaborate preparations were made. A special crew from West Germany orchestrated a worldwide TV hook up. Journalists and religious leaders from all over the world flocked to Uganda. Ugandans of all religious persuasions were ecstatic. Their country was being honored by the visit, not just the Catholic church. In fact, two young Muslims, excited by such a revered and holy personage being in Uganda, jumped into the open car where the Pope was riding just to touch him. The security officers arrested them and reportedly the young men said it did not matter if they died, they had touched God.

A special kitenge cloth made in honor of the visit showed the likenesses of the Pope Paul and President

Obote. The cloth was made into everything, even
umbrellas. The highlight of the visit was the consecration
of site of the shrine to the Uganda Martyrs. These were
twelve young men who, in the 1800s, refused to renounce
Christianity during the rule of a brutal Muslim tribal king.
It was a glorious occasion and all Ugandans were proud to
be granted such an honor.

Meeting the demands of his job and family
obligations caused James to travel a great deal and I missed
him. Edward, teaching, and running the house kept me
busy. Was I homesick? Sure. I recall a day just before my
wedding when a student came to the door and returned a
book he borrowed about Martin Luther King. "They killed
him, madam." "What?," I said. "Dr. King. They killed
him." That was how I found out about the assassination. I
heard about Robert Kennedy's death in a taxi on the way to
Kampala. Even though the radio announcer was speaking
Luganda, I understood enough. In times of great tragedy,
my American juices flowed and I wanted to be there to
share the grief. I really missed my parents and often wished
I could talk with them. Also during my pregnancy, I would
have traded my soul for a pizza with everything. But I had
a good marriage, a beautiful child and lived in a tropical
paradise. Life was good.

Chapter 5
Serpent in the Garden

Monday, January 25, 1971 started like any other day. I arose at 7 a.m. to go to school. James left for Butta the night before and Patrick spent the weekend in Kampala and was expected to report to work that morning. Radio Uganda played only music, no news or morning patter. It was probably the usual transmission problems.

I gathered my books, kissed Edward goodbye; then the phone rang.

"Hello?"

"Sara, it's Patrick calling from Kampala."

"I thought you would be back this morning. Is something wrong?" I queried.

He hesitated. "All night we heard shooting and......I don't know what's happening. I think I'll stay here until we find out what's going on."

My pulse quickened. "I....I hope it's nothing serious."

"Please call the office and tell them I'll be late", he said.

After brief good-byes, I hung up and sat down to assess the situation. President Obote was out of the country

91

at a British Commonwealth Conference in Singapore.
Rumor said that Major General Amin was under house
arrest. The army was most likely making a show of force
and doing a little muscle flexing. I peered out of the
window and saw that the streets seemed a bit more quiet
than usual but there was nothing alarming.

While walking to school, a number of jeeps filled
with armed soldiers whizzed by me. That was unusual
behavior because army personnel rarely left the barracks
with weapons. Still, I was not greatly concerned.

At school, the students buzzed with stories from
their short wave radios of fighting in Entebbe and tanks
surrounding the Parliament building in Kampala. Classes
began, but even these dedicated students were not
interested in the pollination of the hibiscus flower.

Several hours passed with no real change.
Suddenly, the staccato of gunfire erupted from the Jinja
army barracks that sat on a hill just outside of town.
Within ten minutes the school driveway filled with cars as
parents rushed to get their children. School was dismissed
and everyone hurried home to wait for more information.

At home, I tuned in the BBC on short wave. Heavy
fighting was reported in Kampala and Entebbe. The scene
from our front window showed streets filled with jeeps and

trucks rushing back and forth packed with heavily armed troops. I sat on the front steps of the house, watched, and waited. It was
10 a.m.

Time passed slowly. I turned off the BBC when there were no new developments. I tuned in Radio Uganda and listened to the same music that had been playing all day. By 3:45 p.m. there was almost no traffic on the streets. There was an eerie quiet for that time of day. Suddenly a loud explosion shook the windows of the house. It seemed to come from the southwest in an area near the government offices. Almost immediately jeeps loaded with soldiers sped past the house headed in the direction of the explosion.

While my heart still raced from the shock of the explosion, Radio Uganda suddenly came back on the air with these words. "This is Major General Idi Amin Dada. In order to keep a bad situation from becoming worse, the armed forces of Uganda have found it necessary to take over the government." He then proceeded to give fourteen reasons for the coup ranging from nepotism to moral misconduct. He also declared a dusk to dawn curfew. Anyone found on the street between 7 p.m. and 7 a.m. would be shot. The constitution was suspended and parliament disbanded.

Many years have passed since that moment, but I can still see every color and hear every noise. The chilling voice of Idi Amin from the radio, the bright sunshine reflecting off the helmets and guns of the troops as they sped past. I learned that the explosion came from the District Commissioner's house (the same place my parents had stayed during their visit). Amin's troops thought soldiers were hiding there and attacked with mortar shells. Fortunately, no one was inside.

Incredibly, Sweetie Pie was in the middle of a military coup. This was something you heard about on the news or read about somewhere else in the world. But it did not really happen to you, and it definitely was not supposed to happen in stable, happy, idyllic Uganda.

How does a man like Amin could come to power? I do not know. I am not a political analyst or an expert on African affairs. There is no simple answer. One factor is the lingering effect of colonialism. Countries were not prepared for independence but rather thrust into independence by their colonial masters. They were saddled with forms of government and economic structures that suited the needs of the colonizing power. For instance, some of the best farmland is planted in crops like tea, sisal, and coffee while the governments must import corn and wheat for food.

Another major factor is the malady of tribalism. The populace idolizes the first president of a former colony or protectorate. His picture may even be on the currency. When the national anthem is played on television or at the movies, his picture is shown and everyone stands. He molds the government and country to his liking. As a result, most leaders are reluctant to relinquish power and surround themselves with relatives and members of their own tribe. Other tribes are given some positions of authority but the real power stays with a select few. The other tribes begin to believe that the only way to share in the wealth is to overthrow the government, install themselves as rulers, and surround themselves with loyal tribesmen. We see tribalism all over the world. The conflicts in the Middle East and the Balkans are just different varieties of tribalism, one ethnic group pitted against another.

President Obote's enemies wanted him out. An attempt had been made on his life in December of 1969 and he was constantly being accused of tribal favoritism and stockpiling money abroad. Amin was under investigation for involvement in the murder of an army general and smuggling ivory and gold from the Congo. Amin, once a trusted colleague, evidently managed to place officers sympathetic to him in strategic positions in the military.

Another factor that cannot be overlooked is that President Obote was one of the most outspoken supporters of majority African rule in Rhodesia and other white ruled parts of Africa. His speech at the Singapore conference dealt with that subject. This position made him unpopular in some rather powerful circles. Why Amin came to power is not as important as the result of his reign. The chronology of events is unimportant. It is the results of these events that impacted everyone who lived in Uganda.

Immediately after the coup, there was a dichotomy of feelings about and attitudes towards the new regime. Many danced in the streets, sounded auto horns, and decorated their houses and cars in celebration. Obote is gone! Long live Amin! One segment of the population viewed Amin as a kindly, benevolent, simple man who had "liberated" Uganda from the despotic rule of Milton Obote. But a quieter more skeptical segment of the citizenry already doubted the intent of Amin's government.

Patrick arrived that afternoon with stories of roadblocks on the journey from Kampala. "Tanks are everywhere," he said. "The parliament building and Radio Uganda are both surrounded." I prayed that James would stay in Butta until things settled down.

As 7 p.m. approached, the streets emptied. Radio Uganda broadcast music interspersed with announcements about the coup and reminders of the dusk to dawn curfew. The BBC, Voice of America, Radio South Africa, and Deutschewelle all told the same story. Amin controlled the government of Uganda. President Obote found out about the coup on the plane as he returned to Uganda and President Julius Nyerere offered Obote asylum in Tanzania.

The next morning dawned. James had not returned and I hoped he was safe. There was no way to contact him at Butta, but Patrick called Mbale and things were quiet there. I arose to prepare for school and initiated what would become a familiar routine. First listen to Radio Uganda. The entire newscast was "Major General Amin stated.....," "The Commander-in-Chief explained....," "Amin warned......". Then listen to the BBC. "Overnight several people were shot on sight or arrested for violating the curfew. There are also reports of fighting in the barracks between troop loyal to ousted President Obote and supporters of Major General Amin."

Many students stayed home that first day. Those who came talked only of the reports from the BBC and conversations with relatives and friends in other parts of the country. There was sporadic fighting and gunfire, heavy troop movement but very few civilian casualties. Maybe things would be back to normal soon.

Amin's lineage is murky. He alternately claims to be a Kakwa or Lugbara from the northwest corner of Uganda on the Sudan border. Many considered him to be Sudanese and not Ugandan at all. During colonial days, as a member of the Kings African Rifles, Amin was an enforcer. He quelled uprisings with speed and cruelty. Obote believed Amin to be loyal and even felt confident enough to say at one point that he was one of the few African leaders who did not have to worry about a military coup.

During the first few weeks after the coup, Amin promoted more members of his tribe to positions of authority in the army. That meant that large numbers of Langi and Acholi troops, who were loyal to Obote, were under the command of Amin's henchmen. Privates were promoted to major, corporals to colonels, and Amin himself to full general.

Stories about barbaric executions of army personnel suspected of opposing the coup circulated in Uganda and were reported by overseas news agencies. Radio Uganda blamed the reports on imperialists and Obote henchmen. By March, 1971 reports of massacres were too numerous to be ignored. Langi and Acholi tribesmen were reportedly called out for inspection and shot as they stood in their ranks. Massacres were reported at Makindye prison near Kampala, Lira in the north, and in June 1971, Mbarara in western Uganda.

Two American reporters drove to investigate the massacre in Mbarara and never returned. The disappearance of reporters Stroh and Siedel made international news. Army officials at Mbarara denied seeing them. Amin set up a special Commission of Inquiry into their disappearance that found no evidence of wrongdoing. Their remains were found buried in the barracks some years later. But even as the commission did its work, the killings continued.

On July 11, 1971 Amin left Uganda for London. He lunched with the Queen and dined with Prime Minister Heath, assuring the world that "....everything in Uganda was good completely and also." But during his absence, a massacre occurred at the army barracks in Jinja.

The barracks sat on a hill just outside of the city and the road leading to the gate was visible from the town. Just after dawn, a stream of jeeps, trucks and buses flowed along the road going in and out of the barracks. Then the shooting began. From our house, I could hear the chatter of automatic weapon fire, the explosion of grenades, the whistle of artillery shells. Ambulances and jeeps carrying the wounded passed our house en route to the hospital.

I went to school more to find out what was happening than from any sense of duty. Rumors, suppositions, and speculations were myriad: it was another coup, Entebbe airport had been taken over, Obote was back. No one really knew anything for certain. School began and we tried to conduct classes as normal. Fearing stray bullets, we kept the girls inside and canceled all sports activities.

Suddenly, with spinning tires and squealing brakes an army jeep roared into the school driveway. Two heavily armed soldiers in bloodstained uniforms, leaped out of the jeep and raced up the stairs to the top of the school clock tower. For a few minutes they observed the barracks through binoculars and then left as abruptly as they had come. They never said a word to anyone. Minutes later, the sound of a tremendous explosion erupted from the barracks, followed by heavy automatic weapons fire. At school, all semblance of order was lost. The school driveway filled with cars as hysterical parents came for their children. Girls were screaming and crying. School was dismissed.

Radio Uganda, quoted a "government spokesman" as saying that "target practice and training exercises" were going on in the Jinja barracks and there was no cause for alarm. The most reliable explanation of that day's events was this. All Langi and Acholi in the Jinja barracks were ordered killed. The troops were called out to line up for inspection and then shot down in cold blood. A few managed to escape and barricaded themselves in the ammunition depot, a two-story cement block structure. The trapped soldiers fired from the windows on the second floor. Those bullets traveled off the hilltop into town and killed several innocent civilians. In an attempt to dislodge the "rebels", Amin's troops brought tanks up to the building and fired. They finally destroyed the building, ignited the ammunition, hence the explosion.

After the massacre, buses and trucks left the barracks carrying the families of the slain soldiers to the train stations. They knew nothing of the fate of their husbands, brothers and fathers. Their questions were answered with blows from gun butts. Later in the day, army personnel commandeered all of the trucks from the Jinja Municipal Council and took them to the barracks. Traffic on the main roads entering and leaving Jinja was stopped. The slain soldiers were loaded into the trucks, taken down

101

and dumped into the Nile. It was said that Amin sent all of his enemies on vacation. He gave them a one way ticket to Cairo.....by sea.

There were reports, later confirmed by eyewitnesses, that in the Langi and Acholi districts of northern Uganda civilians were killed by the thousands. Many men between the ages of sixteen and sixty were arrested, tortured and killed. Those who could, ran away to other parts of the country or to other countries. Soon those areas of the country became a strange land where you could travel for miles and see nothing but young boys, women and the elderly.

Fear became a way of life. It was present every hour of every day. The killings began with the Langi and Acholi and spread to anyone Amin or his cohorts thought needed to be eliminated. You could be arrested for anything, anytime. If you were not officially arrested, you could be kidnapped, taken by force from your home, your office, the street, anywhere. There was no court, no lawyer. You just disappeared never to be seen again...at least not alive.

The perpetrators of these disappearances were members of the army, or State Research Bureau or military police; all of whom directly or indirectly reported to Amin. The victims, bound and gagged, were stuffed into car trunks or jeeps and driven away. Their bodies would be found dumped in the Nile, in the forest, or along the road. These abductions often happened in public places such as bars, hotels, and schools. Even if the license number of the vehicle used was known, nothing would be done. In fact, you were risking your life to get involved.

Amin released numerous political prisoners held for many years by Obote. He encouraged them to become active again because in five years, the army would hand over control to civilians. Pledging political freedom, he smiled and shook their hands and within a year most of them were dead or in forced exile.

Before Amin, the Uganda Police dealt with civilian problems (murder, robbery, traffic etc.) and the military police disciplined the army. The army only entered in civilian matters when the situation was too much for the police, such as the attempted assassination of President Obote in 1969. The army in pre-Amin Uganda was swift and often brutal but their contact with civilians was limited. Occasionally, an army vehicle ran a car off the road, or an army roadblock set up to check for stolen cars roughed up a taxi driver, but these incidents were rare. Post-Amin Uganda was a different story. The army ran everything. The Uganda Police feared the army just like everyone else and the Military Police harassed civilians rather than military personnel. Roadblocks were used to rob, harass and brutalize. There were so many stories and so much fear.

When Nathan began to tell his story, he spoke so softly we leaned forward to hear him. It was as though he feared someone was outside our living room window listening and would rush in if he told us happened.

He was at home when the soldiers came. They dragged him away from his hysterical wife and terrified children, threw him in the back of a Land Rover and stood on him. He had nothing. He was not an important man, just a distant relative of one of Obote's cabinet ministers. Maybe that was why they took him, not that they needed a reason. The Land Rover rumbled on to other houses. Nathan could hardly breathe as other bodies were piled on top of him. They were all praying, crying, pleading. The air soon reeked of ammonia as their bladders reacted to the fear.

Finally, they stopped and pulled Nathan and the others out and threw them on the ground. In the darkness, Nathan could hear water. They were near the Nile River. He could hear others screaming but was afraid to lift his head to see what was happening. He heard laughter as the soldiers approached and stood over him making jokes about the means of his death.

The whistle of the whip vibrated through the air before he felt the thongs cut through his clothes and skin. He screamed in agony as the whip fell again and again. Through the pain he felt wetness covering his body and his nose caught the familiar odor of gasoline. The matches flashed and flared but the wind blew them out before they ignited the gas. He prayed.

Again the victims were piled into the Land Rover. This time Nathan was near the top so he could at least breathe. They traveled to a military base and were locked in a cell where they were forced to lie down in the cold, dirty water.

During the next few days, the soldiers came many times, beat them, kicked them, and whipped them. Pain and agony had no meaning for Nathan. He was beyond that. Some of his cellmates died and were dragged out like fallen cattle. Whenever they heard the soldiers coming, Nathan and his fellow victims dropped down into the filthy, bloody water. If you stood, you paid dearly. But Nathan finally drifted beyond fear or caring and the last time they came, he stood. The soldiers grabbed him and pushed his face against the wall. But he wanted to face them, to watch his death come. As he turned, he heard the whistle of the whip and felt it catch the corner of his eye. Blessed darkness closed in as he sank to the floor. "Thank you God for letting me die. Katonda, Webale".

It must be a dream, Nathan thought. The soft, soothing voice calling his name and the gentle hands helping him to his feet. With his one good eye he focused and saw a familiar face, but Nathan's foggy, confused mind could not connect it with a name. Nathan was led out of the cell and pushed gently on to the rear floor of the car. The rescuer tenderly covered Nathan with a blanket and told him to be quiet. He lay on the floor shivering, trying to understand. Suddenly, he remembered that his savior was an army officer, one of the few reasonable ones. The front door of the car opened and Nathan heard the soft, friendly voice warn him again to be quiet. The car stopped at the front gate and Nathan could hear the guards laughing and joking with the driver. Then they were moving again. Nathan was out. He was free. "Thank you God. Katonda, Webale ". The whip marks on his back, the jagged scar from the corner of his left eye to the jawbone still remain. His soul still bleeds and the fear will be with him forever.

Ben had once been in the army, but resigned before the coup. He kept a low profile after the takeover and tried to live a simple quiet life. One evening as he sat in a hotel having a drink with friends, they came; three men driving in a Peugeot 504. They grabbed Ben and dragged him out, screaming as he was stuffed in the trunk. No one tried to help. No one interfered. Some turned their backs and pretended they did not see. Ben's mind raced. They could be taking him to prison or out into the forest to be killed. He wondered why he had been picked up. But you really did not have to do anything. Terrorism invariably becomes random. He hoped his brother would take care of the wife and children he left behind. He was a solider and ready to die. He only prayed they would not torture him too much. When the trunk opened, he was inside Makindye Prison near Kampala. His watch and ring were placed in a large basket nearly filled with other jewelry. Ben wondered if any of the owners were still alive.

As soon as he entered the cellblock, the smell of fear and death overtook him. Blood, urine, sweat, and decaying flesh, all these odors merged together and assaulted his senses. He was put in a cell with four other men who had been there varying lengths of times, two days, a week, four months. All had been beaten, one tortured. None of them thought they would see the outside world again.

107

The next afternoon, the soldiers came shouting and cursing as they opened the cells and selected victims. Some begged and pleaded. Others silently faced their fate and some stared out of fear-glazed eyes. They took Ben too. All of them were lined up in an open courtyard near the center of the prison. First, they selected one man, made him lie down, and tied his hands and feet to stakes in the ground. While he pleaded for his life, a solider with an axe began his work. Feet were severed first, then knees, hip joints, wrists, shoulders, head. Ben stood in horrified silence. Others prayed, vomited, cried, or screamed in terror. Ben was returned to his cell untouched. But some were kept behind. He could hear their screams and the sadistic laughter of their torturers. When the screaming stopped, they came for him again. Ben and several others carried the butchered bodies and piled them on the back of a truck. As they did their gruesome work, their jailers taunted them, "You will be next."

The same procedure with only slight variation was repeated many times. Ben was taken from his cell to witness murders or to move bodies or to wash up blood. He saw prisoners pitted against each other. One would be told to kill another with a promise of immunity from punishment. They bludgeoned each other with sledgehammers or stabbed each other, thinking their crime would save their lives. But all too often, their captors also killed them. But Ben was always spared. Eight weeks after being picked up, he was just as inexplicably released.

Ben went into hiding at his home in the countryside. When you were with him, you would catch him staring out into space with a blank, vacant expression in his eyes. You knew he would never be the same again.

The army reigned supreme. They could do anything they wanted to do. If they wanted your house or car they took them. If they wanted your wife they killed you and took her. Laws changed at Amin's whim and were usually announced at 5 p.m.on the radio news broadcast:

With immediate effect, the constitution is suspended and parliament is disbanded.

With immediate effect, all civilians with guns must turn them in to the army. Any civilian caught with a firearm will be arrested.

With immediate effect the news will be broadcast in Arabic, French and Swahili as well as English.

With immediate effect, women cannot wear make-up or wigs.

Wearing the special kitenge cloth made for the visit of the Pope became a death warrant because it had Obote's picture on it. Shirts, dresses, and umbrellas were burned or buried. I saw a young man, a Makerere student, nearly shot because he had a Uganda history book that included a picture of Obote.

To the rest of the world Amin was a buffoon who said and did outrageous things. He outfitted an entire regiment in kilts. He bought amphibious tanks and organized a navy in a land locked country with an army that could not swim. He said things like "I thank you from the bottom of my heart and my wife's bottom also." Or "I propose getting rid of conventional armaments and replacing them with reasonably priced hydrogen bombs that would be distributed equally throughout the world." He awarded himself a chest full of medals and wore them all. He awarded himself a degree in political science from Makerere University. As President, Amin was Chancellor of Makerere University. When he handed out degrees, the degree categories were spelled out phonetically so that he could pronounce them correctly. Still he would say things like "I confer upon you the degree of "emoconics" instead of economics or "sugary" instead of surgery. He did not even attempt to say obstetrics and gynecology.

My most frightening experience occurred on a day when James was in Butta. My mother-in-law had gone to

Kampala for a visit. Late that morning, a friend in Mbale called, saying that James had been spotted tied up in the back of a Land Rover entering an army base near Mbale. I got word to my mother-in-law and brother-in-law Patrick. Within two hours we were on our way to Mbale.

All the way there an eerie silence filled the car. We all had the same unexpressed thoughts. What if James was dead? If the army had him we would never see him again or find his body. My imagination ran rampant. Had he been tortured? Had he died slowly? It was the longest car ride of my life.

We arrived at Butta just after dark. A neighbor's young daughter sat alone on the front porch. We asked her where James was. She said he left earlier in the day and had not said where he was going. Our hearts sank. It must have been him on the Land Rover. They had him. As we sat silent, wondering what to do next, we heard footsteps and James rushed in through the back door. He had been at a neighbor's house working. Seeing Patrick's car he thought something had happened to Edward or me. He was as frightened as we were. The man in the Land Rover, a cousin who bore a strong resemblance to James, was never seen again.

Chapter 6
Passports, Asians and Magendo

When I decided to stay in Uganda, I knew I would
eventually face the monumental decision of whether or not
to become a Uganda citizen. Even under Obote, it was
more and more difficult for non-citizens to get jobs or start
businesses. With James attempting to get a loan to start his
farm, I knew that our financial situation would demand that
I work. After the coup, I was concerned about putting
James and his family in danger by having an "imperialist"
in the family.

I understood that renouncing my American
citizenship deprived me of some important options. If I
wanted to go to the United States even for a visit, I would
have to get a visa. If I wanted to return for good, I would be
treated as an immigrant.

It took many hours of thought and soul searching
and it was one of the most difficult decisions I have ever
made, especially with Amin in power. But in mid-1972,
four months pregnant with our second child, I renounced
my American citizenship and became a Uganda citizen.
The officer at the American Embassy was very kind. He

questioned me at length and explained all of the
ramifications of my decision. He also told me that I could
sign a confidential document saying that I was forced to
renounce my citizenship. I did not sign for two reasons.
First, I was not being forced to do anything. Second,
"confidential" documents like that in the wrong hands
could be deadly. He gave me a copy of the renunciation and
said he would not process my papers for a few days in case
I changed my mind. I did not.

I am often asked if I became a Uganda citizen
because I was disillusioned with America. If growing up
poor and black in Chicago had not disillusioned me, four
years in Africa certainly would not. I held no animosity
toward the United States. I understood and appreciated the
wonderful things about my country. However, I had to
survive the situation in which I found myself. In my mind,
the best way to do that was to be inconspicuous and non-
controversial. Not only my fate, but also the fate of my
husband, children and in-laws might depend on the color of
my passport. Obtaining Uganda citizenship documents was
one of the wisest decision I ever made. In October, 1972 I
got a job with the East African Community, a job that
would allow me to travel to Kenya and Tanzania and paid a
fairly high wage. Years later when I tried to get proof of

my renunciation, none could be found. Either the officer never filed it or it was lost when the American embassy was hurriedly closed a year later.

On December 17, 1972 our daughter was born. She was named Lillian Leah Lumonya Wanambwa; Lillian for my aunt who accompanied my parents to our wedding, Leah for her maternal great-grandmother and Lumonya for a great aunt. Lillian has always been very calm. She does not get excited easily and takes things pretty much as they come. Perhaps this is because she was born at a time of such great turmoil.

On August 5, 1972 President Amin announced that all people of Asian descent who were not Uganda citizens must leave Uganda within ninety days. Amin had "spoken with God" who told him that Asians had to go. Amin said the Asians made money in Uganda and stockpiled it in banks overseas. He accused them of using Uganda's economy: "They milked the cow but didn't feed it."

The Asians (Indians and Pakistanis) originally came to East Africa to help build the railroad from the coast at Mombassa, Kenya inland to Uganda. They were astute businessmen and opened shops and factories. They sent for their relatives and continued to prosper. Although the Asians had been in East Africa for many years, they were still very much a separate community. There was little intermarriage with Ugandans. Most Asians only spoke broken Swahili, few had learned the vernacular of the area where they lived. They spoke Hindi, Gujerati, or other languages only they understood. They imported their own Asian movies and even maintained their own schools as much as possible. Their attitude towards Africans was often patronizing or exploitative. No one can deny the economic contributions Asians made to Uganda, but there were a group subject to suspicion, criticism and resentment. This was fertile ground for Amin's exploitative mind.

When Uganda became independent, the British government gave the Asians several options. They could retain their Indian or Pakistani passports, become Uganda citizens, or be issued a British passport. Many opted for the "security" of British citizenship. The British passports they were issued had a D in front of the passport number. In some Asian families, you found one person with an Indian passport, one with a Uganda passport and another with a British passport. All bets were covered. The August announcement said that within ninety days all Asians who were not Uganda citizens must leave. The only exceptions were teachers, lawyers, and other professionals. All businessmen must itemize their assets and turn them over to the government. The exodus would begin in September. Amin failed to plug up all the loopholes and the Asians immediately began sending money out of Uganda. Gold, usually in the form of jewelry, was smuggled out in cars, bags of produce, even in a dead body. Cars purchased with Uganda currency were driven to Kenya and sold for Kenya currency that was more valuable. Purchase orders were obtained from connections overseas. Uganda currency was converted to foreign money to pay for the goods. The goods never arrived.

The Asians registered with the government to determine their citizenship and to be issued identification cards. It was an exercise in humiliation. Men, women and children stood in line for hours outside of the Immigration Department in Kampala. They were "guarded" by army personnel who took every opportunity to degrade them. Those who were Uganda citizens had been told they were exempt from the expulsion order. Amin changed his mind again and said that all Asians had to go. He then changed his mind again and said that Uganda citizens could stay. By then all Asians, citizens , professionals, and non-citizens were frantic to leave.

Amin then dealt the final blow. He announced that once Asians had purchased airline tickets they had only twenty-four hours to leave the country. Panic ensued. The Asians sold everything they could, even their prized personal possessions. It was heartbreaking to see people with their front doors open calling strangers in off the street to buy their household goods, to see businesses that had been built up over several generations abandoned, some of them fully stocked. Cars even Mercedes, Audis and Peugeots were sold for a few hundred dollars. Tractors and eighteen wheelers were almost given away. Amin promised the Asians they would be allowed to take their money with them and be paid a fair price for their businesses and houses. But the promise meant nothing. Each family was only allowed to take a small amount of money in foreign currency, leaving behind their lives works and savings. Heartbreak, desperation, anger, deceit, hopelessness was reflected in their faces. At the airport, a small Asian child seen carrying an airline bag that seemed unusually heavy. It was found to be filled with gold. An Asian woman with a cast on her arm used her "broken" arm to lift a suitcase. The cast was removed to reveal an arm full of gold bracelets. An older Asian woman was carrying an unusually heavy container of food and inside the cupcakes were rings and jewels.

Some of the cars and trucks bought from the Asians

117

at giveaway prices suddenly stopped working. The departing owners put sugar in the gas tanks that ruined the engines. An Asian businessman, frustrated over not being able to exchange his Uganda money for usable currency, burned stacks of currency in his back yard. Asians with Uganda passports, terrified of being left behind, destroyed their passports, escaped to Kenya and declared themselves stateless. They claimed the Uganda government confiscated or destroyed their passports which was often true. Houses and shops lay abandoned and ransacked. Factories were shut down and distribution of goods was totally disrupted. Families whose members had different passports were separated. Our Lillian Leah Lumonya Wanambwa was born into a country about to self-destruct.

Asians with British D passports faced more hardship once they left Uganda. They were refused entry to India and Pakistan. But their greatest shock came when they were refused entry to Britain. The British government said those with D passports were on a quota system and would be put on a waiting list. Since the airline that brought them was responsible, they flew to country after country and were refused entry everywhere. Other countries were understandably hesitant to admit people whose own country had rejected them. Likewise, the "stateless" Asians with no passports were shuttled all over the world. A few were admitted to Canada, the United States and a few other countries, but the majority were stranded.

Britain became the object of international scrutiny. Australians, Rhodesians, New Zealanders and other white immigrants were not on a quota system. Britain faced racial unrest with its large Jamaican and West Indian populations and the government could only see an increase in tension with an influx of Asians. But finally Britain gave in and admitted all persons with D passports.

To many Asians, Uganda was the only home they had ever known and India or Britain were just places to visit. The more compassionate Ugandans felt that if the Asians should be given a fair price for their possessions and businesses. To force them to leave it all behind was horrendous. Amin's loyal following believed that wholesale expulsion of Asians was a good thing. Amin was giving the country back to Ugandans. Now everyone would have a business and a big house and lots of money. Amin was hero, savior, and liberator.

To complicate matters even more, on the day the first Asians left, Milton Obote, the deposed president, led an invasion of Uganda from Tanzania. The invasion failed miserably and Amin's revenge was brutal. He massacred many of invaders and imprisoned the rest. The battle between Amin's troops and the invasion force continued for several days. Both civilian and military casualties were heavy and stories of atrocities plentiful. Near the town of Masaka, Ugandan troops indiscriminately killed anyone they suspected of "collaboration with the enemy". People were disemboweled and decapitated. One local chief's genitals were cut off and stuffed into his mouth as he hung from a tree. The newspaper pictures of piles of bodies and lines of prisoners were gruesome. The invaders were repulsed. We never knew exactly what caused the invasion to fail, but it was rumored that the invading force took a wrong turn and allowed Amin's troops to drive a wedge between their units. Whatever the reason, the "liberation army" retreated into Tanzania, leaving behind many prisoners who would die horrible deaths in Ugandan prisons.

One of those captured was Pico Ali, a long time Obote ally. He and a captured colleague, were taken to see Amin who welcomed them warmly, served refreshments and said he did not hate them. They were then allegedly beaten to death by soldiers. It was reported by a government spokesman that with the help of other "guerrillas", Pico Ali and his companion had escaped and gone back to Tanzania.

But the worst result of the unsuccessful invasion was the effect on Amin. He became totally paranoid. Everyone was his enemy. Everyone was a guerrilla. Now there was a valid excuse to arrest, torture and kill. After the invasion, everything that went wrong in Uganda was blamed on guerrillas from Tanzania, particularly guerrillas trained by exiled President Obote. The guerillas kidnapped prominent people. Unfavorable stories in the foreign press were guerrilla propaganda. Guerrillas sabotaged the economy causing shortages of essential commodities. Exactly how they did this was never clarified. Whenever Amin wanted to detract attention from his own activities, he would predict an imminent invasion from Tanzania. He even advised people to gather stones to throw at enemy planes.

Uganda lost most of its most educated citizens during this time. They were picked up and never seen again. Educators, doctors, lawyers, businessmen, the people whom Uganda most needed, succumbed to Amin's savagery or had to run for their lives.

Benedicto Kiwanuka, a highly educated, well-respected judge, was the Chief Justice of Uganda. Kiwanuka openly criticized some of Amin's activities.

Two specific incidents were cited. A group of men who
attempted to steal a hospital payroll were captured by the
army, marched into an open field and executed. Justice
Kiwanuka reportedly told Amin that if the men were guilty
they should have brought to trial. If the army was going to
be judge and jury then the courts had no function. The
second incident involved a British businessman who Amin
had arrested and held without charge for several days.
Justice Kiwanuka, after receiving complaints from the
British government, ordered that the man either be charged
or released. Amin ordered the man's deportation within
twenty-four hours. Again Kiwanuka complained. He felt
the powers and functions of the courts were being usurped.
His integrity was to be his undoing.

During the invasion from Tanzania and for almost a
week afterwards, all roads to and from Kampala were
heavily guarded. No one got in or out of the city without
passing through numerous roadblocks. On September 21,
1972 men wearing Uganda Army uniforms entered a
Kampala courtroom and removed Benedicto Kiwanuka. He
was handcuffed, blindfolded and made to remove his shoes.
Chief Justice Kiwanuka was never seen again.

The official government story stated that guerrillas
somehow penetrated the tight security net, kidnapped

Kiwanuka and took him out of Kampala. How Benedicto Kiwanuka died is a matter of speculation. Some say he was tortured and shot. Others reported that he was placed in a steel drum half filled with oil and boiled alive. Whatever the real story, he surely met a horrible end.

Amin alleged at one point that Chinese troops were lined up along the Tanzanian border ready to attack. There were often shots fires across the border. During one of these skirmishes a Tanzanian police officer was killed and Ugandan soldiers took his body. The officer was half-German and half-Tanzanian. His physical features clearly reflected his heritage but Amin claimed the man was a colonel in the Chinese army. To prove his allegation he put the handcuffed dead body on display at Kololo airstrip in Kampala and published a picture of the "colonel' on the front page of the newspaper.

On the economic front the situation was dismal. The Asians were gone. The army or high-ranking officials took the best houses and shops and most of the businesses were closed. The dilemma faced by Amin was how and to whom to distribute the businesses and houses left by the expelled Asians. He solved this with his usual flair by declaring the Economic War.

If you wanted a house or business, you stood in

front of that house or business on the day the Allocation Committee came by. The committee was composed of army, police and prison services officers. They would choose one of the crowd, more or less at random. Those chosen become instant entrepreneurs or homeowners. James and I tried to get a house but found that the best houses were already spoken for and the houses that remained needed major repairs. We did not even try to get a business because by then we knew enough to be sure it was a risky venture at best.

Some of the shops were fully stocked and even had cash boxes full of money which the Asians, in their haste, had left while other shops had been ransacked. This novel method of distributing businesses meant that many of the people who got shops knew nothing about how to run a business and some were barely literate. There were many Ugandans with enough business acumen to be successful, but too often the determining factor in the ownership of a business was who you knew on the Allocation Committee or just pure chance. The results were tragically amusing. I went to town a few days after the shops reopened. I asked the price of a shirt and was told fourteen shillings, the equivalent of $2.00. I was dumfounded. Another shirt was priced at 15 shillings. When I remarked about the low price, the proprietor showed me the "price tag." It was actually a label showing the neck size.

Because the shops had been closed for as long as six or eight months, and prices were often ridiculously low, a large amount of merchandise was sold in a short time. The new shop owners became "rich" overnight. These businessmen were dubbed Mafuta Mingi by Amin which means "much fat". Because many were inexperienced or uneducated, little thought was given to how the money should be best used. Unfortunately, many of the Mafuta Mingi regarded all of the money as profit. The results, initially hilarious, were ultimately devastating.

A newly affluent Mafuta Mingi would enter a hotel or bar and say that everyone could eat or drink as much as they wished he would pay. When the bill was presented, the waiter would be given the key to the trunk of the Mafuta's car. The trunk would be full of money and the waiter could remove the amount he thought sufficient. Entire floors in hotels were reserved and family and friends would be invited to stay, eat and drink. They bought clothes, cars, jewelry, all the luxuries that were unobtainable before.

The international money market has always been a puzzle to me but one aspect of it must be understood to follow what happened in Uganda. Americans are accustomed to having their money accepted anywhere in the world. This is not true for countries like Uganda. In order to purchase goods that they do not manufacture, these countries must sell their raw materials or other products to European, North American, or Asian countries and use that money to buy what is needed. This, in a simplified way, is foreign exchange.

The use of foreign exchange was always a tightly regulated process in Uganda. To purchase goods from abroad, a business owner:

1.   Obtained a pro forma invoice from the supplier stating what items were to be bought and their exact cost.

2.   Submitted this invoice to the Bank of Uganda and possibly waited a considerable amount of time for the funds to become available.

3.   Proved receipt of the goods after they arrived. The Bank of Uganda sent payment directly to the supplier.

Under Amin, this system was abandoned. The new system was capricious favoritism. If you were a Mafuta Mingi, a Muslim, an army officer, or a member of the right

126

tribe, you could get just about whatever you wanted. Uganda currency was changed to pounds, francs, and dollars in huge amounts and issued to those "preferred customers" for purchasing goods abroad. The strict system of checks and accountability was gone. The money was just handed to the requesters who never had to account for how it was used.

After obtaining foreign currency, the Mafutas, Muslims, and military personnel went abroad and purchased luxury items for themselves or just banked the money. They might purchase a few goods to stock their shops in Uganda, but most of the money was squandered on personal items.

The results were predictable. The supply of goods left by the Asians soon dwindled and no new goods were brought in to replenish the declining supply. Foreign exchange coffers were very low or empty. No spare parts, no clothes, no medicine because of no foreign exchange. One high ranking government official was heard to remark in Swahili, "Where is this foreign change (sic)? Why can't we find him? Where is his office? Surely, we can get him and make him order all the things we need. How can we let one man make so much trouble?" A clear case of failure to grasp the concept.

127

The few goods available soon became objects of fierce competition. Uganda money had no value even in Uganda. Prices soared and the black market flourished. It even had its own name, magendo. You could not buy things at the stores but you could get them magendo. The government issued an official price list but you could never find things at those prices. Amin threatened to jail anyone who sold at magendo prices and occasionally the Military Police would storm through town and close shops whose prices were not at government levels.

Whenever you went to town you never knew what you would find or which commodities would be available. Salt, sugar, flour, toilet paper, bread, butter, milk, all appeared and disappeared randomly.

The "Redtops", as the Military Police were called because of their red hats, would even stop people on the street and ask how much they paid for the items they were carrying. If they said they bought it on the black market they were beaten or forced to eat the soap or salt or whatever they had. If they said they paid the government price they were not believed and beaten anyway. Magendo flourished; sugar was $8.00/lb, cigarettes $10/pack, salt $2/lb, milk $2/pint, soap $2/bar. If a store received a shipment of salt or sugar and was forced to sell at the

128

government price, the line would be three blocks long and you had to bring your own paper bag. Children earned large sums by standing in line for people. Large crowds followed the truck distributing the sugar and lined up even before the goods were unloaded. Shops began to close or were abandoned. The rent and utility payments due the government by the Mafuta Mingi were never sent. Hospitals ran out of medicine. Factories closed. Transportation was impossible. Buses and taxis were few because of fuel shortages and lack of spare parts. Traveling from Jinja to Kampala was and all day frustration. Buses would be packed beyond capacity with four people on a seat and the aisles jammed. Taxis would stop in the taxi park and say they were not going to make another trip. Suddenly they would begin shouting "Kampala, Kampala, Kampala" sparking a mad rush as people struggled to get one of the seven seats. The taxi fares quadrupled.

Finally came the industrial collapse. Production rates and quality fell. There was dirty, brown, burned sugar, bread with pieces of flour sack baked in it and no beer because there were no caps or bottles. The price of a bottle of beer rose from $.25 to $3.00 to up to $14.25 a bottle, magendo price. It was common practice that those who worked at a factory received a free ration of whatever they produced, sugar, oil, soap, candy, etc. Now they worked all day for worthless money then went to town and paid outrageous prices for the goods they worked to produce. Workers showed their anger by sabotaging machinery or setting acres of sugar cane on fire. It was rumored that sugar and meat and cooking oil was being shipped out to Libya and other Arab countries in exchange for arms. Truckloads of goods would disappear between the factories and the depots in the city. There were rumors of stockpiling by the army, but for ordinary Ugandans, the net result was deprivation and desperation.

The hospitals became chambers of horrors. There was no medicine, few doctors, vermin, and overcrowding. There was no salt and sugar to make saline solution for dehydration, no antibiotics and no surgeons to operate. Uganda was dying.

Life under a government run by the Uganda Army was never dull. Frightening, infuriating, dangerous, unpredictable, violent even comical but never dull. As soon as Amin seized power, he began promoting Muslims, and members of his tribe. Privates were promoted to colonel, sergeants to majors etc. Many of them could hardly read or write. They bought or commandeered all of the luxuries their new position afforded; cars, houses, stereos, clothes, watches, radios, TVs. They decorated their cars with curtains, Venetian blinds, stuffed animals and musical horns. They bought three piece suits, bell-bottomed blue jeans, and sunglasses. It was a common sight in the once posh hotels to see the new leadership using curtains, tablecloths, and furniture covers as napkins. They were sent overseas as ambassadors and students and the reports that came back were humiliating. Those sent to pilots training were sent home because they could not read or write. A new ambassador arrived at this post and, for the first time, saw a door with an electric eye. It opened automatically as he approached and he jumped back in surprise. When the phenomenon was explained, he proceeded to run back and forth through the door like a child. Many wore two or more watches but could not tell time. They wore rings, chains, necklaces, etc. in profusion. After the Asians left, some army personnel obtained numerous cars. One, the Provincial Governor of the Central Province, had twenty-six cars. He would often change cars six or seven times a day. The cars were usually wrecked as quickly as they were obtained. Every week three or four of Amin's people died in a fiery crash usually caused by excessive speed and recklessness.

Surprisingly the cabinet that Amin initially chose

was one of the most qualified in Africa. He had men from many tribes who were well educated, experienced and devoted to their country. But within two years most had been killed, dismissed or left the country. Some left because they were in danger, some because their consciences would not allow them to stay.

The dimensions of the military government's mismanagement and ignorance were limitless: The Army Chief of Staff could not read or write and could not answer or carry on an intelligent conversation on the telephone. He had an aide who answered the phone and relayed his replies to the caller.

In Jinja, a vehicle belonging to a certain factory broke down. The driver returned to the plant, requisitioned another truck, and took along a technician to help him repair the stalled vehicle. At the gate the guard duly recorded that the driver left with a truck and a mechanic. The next day the twenty-year-old army captain who managed the plant accused the driver of stealing machinery. The captain thought the "mechanic" listed in the guard's report was a piece of equipment.

A commonly repeated story involved Amin's original Minister of Finance, a highly qualified man, who informed the president that Uganda's foreign reserves were very low and that the country would soon have no money. Amin reportedly slapped him, drove him to the Bank of Uganda to show him a vault full of worthless Uganda money. How could Uganda be broke with all that money?

Trips to the open market, once such a joyous adventure, became an ordeal. Lack of spare parts and tires and gasoline made transportation difficult. Produce from the villages was scarce so prices soared. Matoke, while still available, tripled in price. Many days no meat was available.

The government did not pay its bills. Being landlocked everything came into to Uganda through another country. Uganda's gasoline came from refineries in Mombassa, Kenya. In the morass that was Uganda, the oil companies were not paid for several months and stopped all gasoline shipments.

Amin was outraged. He boasted that he had friends in the Arab world who would send him all the crude oil he wanted. Exactly how the crude oil would become gasoline was unclear. Amin threatened Kenya with military force and diplomatic pressure. Kenya replied that the answer was simple: if you pay the gas will come. Tankers passing thorough Uganda bound for Rwanda and Burundi were highjacked by the army. After several drivers endured severe beatings, no one dared enter Uganda with anything carrying gasoline. The country came to a standstill, literally.

You could walk down the middle of the main street in Jinja at high noon and see no buses, no taxis, no cars, no trucks, nothing. Only a few army vehicles moved through the streets. Patients arrived at the hospital in wheelbarrows. Goods became even scarcer and more outrageously expensive. After a few weeks, Amin finally paid the bill and things started to move again. But this episode only served to accelerate the inevitable demise of Uganda.

A simple evening out for dinner and drinks became a struggle. "In order to reduce drunkenness and promote the principles of Islam," the government restricted bar hours. Bars opened at 12:30 p.m. and closed at 2 p.m. They reopened at
5 p.m. and closed again at 10 p.m. No ingredients, no caps, no bottles etc. made beer and even Uganda Waragi scarce. Bars once stocked with imported wines and liquors were now bare. Beer often arrived just as the bar opened. Transported on open trucks, the bottles were almost too hot to touch and would often explode while being unloaded. But we drank it anyway.

Bars and hotels went to extremes to conserve the beer supply. Some places refused to serve anyone who was not seated and then removed half the chairs. Others would only serve each person one beer at a time and you had to hand in the empty bottle to get another one. The easiest way to circumvent this arrangement was to sit in a large group and have each person finish at a different time. The waiter retrieved one bottle and when he brought the refill another person handed him an empty bottle. When that refill came another person was ready. The waiter soon tired of the drill and brought as much beer as he could at one time.

Restaurants had no menus and served what was available on that day. They often ran out of food. The elaborate high teas were no more, you were lucky to get plain bread. Beautiful Uganda, the Pearl of Africa, the Garden of Eden lay in ruins at the feet of a madman.

Chapter 7

The Deadly Keystone Cops

Amin became fascinated with Scotland, Ireland and Wales. He felt that the British exploited them, like Uganda. As a show of solidarity with their "struggle against imperialism" he outfitted an entire regiment in kilts at considerable expense. He also wanted to buy them bear skin hats like the guards at Buckingham Palace wear, but was finally convinced that the climate was too damp and hot to maintain the fur.

After breaking ties with the West, Amin bought large amounts of military paraphernalia from Russia. Even the untrained eye could tell that the equipment was second hand with a new coat of paint. The jeeps broke down and spare parts were not available. The gaskets for Russian trucks were almost an inch thick rather that the usual dime thinness. He bought amphibious tanks for use in Lake Victoria near Jinja. The tanks malfunctioned or sank. Amin even organized a Uganda Navy in a landlocked country. Among the military hardware purchased by Amin were two snowplows.

The military jets were toys for Amin's pilots. Since

Uganda is so small, the only way the jets could reach supersonic speed without entering a neighboring country's air space was to climb and dive straight down. One jet jockey decided to do acrobatics while diving over Lake Victoria. Blue sky up, blue water down. Which way was up? He made the wrong choice and dove at supersonic speed into the lake. It took several weeks before the plane and what was left of the pilot rose to the surface. Another pilot buzzed the home of his girlfriend and while waving and waggling his wings, flew into the side of a mountain. Most of the remaining jets lay disabled from lack of spare parts.

Before Amin, you never saw military personnel in uniform in a bar. But after "liberation" it was the rule rather than the exception. Fights between army people and civilians became common. A military person might take any innocent comment as a personal affront. People were beaten up or killed for bumping against a table, spilling a drink, talking to a barmaid whom the army man considered to be his girlfriend. Friendly dances that James and I used to attend on Saturdays in the Jinja town hall became brawls with flying bottles and bullets. If you were abused by army personnel, you had no one to complain to, no where to go, no recourse. You took your punishment and were grateful to be left alive.

The government controlled the newspapers, radio and television. You could sit with a copy of the Voice of Uganda and listen to a newscast that would mirror the newspaper account exactly. Vernacular newspapers, particularly those written in Luganda, attempted to print a more accurate account of events but eventually were brought to heel. Amin even demanded that they stop using such complicated language because he could not understand it.

In June 1974 all newspapers and magazines not published in Uganda were banned and to be caught with a foreign publication meant death. A friend of ours went on a business trip to Kenya and innocently wrapped his shoes in a Kenya newspaper when he packed. He was arrested at the border and accused of being an imperialist spy. Fortunately, he managed to bribe his way out of the situation.

The Defense Council, The Public Safety unit, The State Research Bureau, all of these were euphemistic titles for goon squads. Those who comprised these groups made decisions on everything from dress codes to foreign policy. Their word was law. If they ordered your arrest or criticized your work of behavior, your days were numbered. No one was immune, military personnel,

Cabinet ministers, clergy, were all subject to their scrutiny.

Another horror came in February of 1973 when Amin ordered public executions. At various locations around Uganda, men were publicly shot for crimes ranging from treason to black market activities. None of them had been convicted in court. One was a fifteen-year old school boy. The army stormed through towns closed all the businesses and forced people to attend the executions. Army men dressed in camouflage gear with their faces hidden were on the firing squads. Film of the executions was shown on the evening news and pictures were printed in the newspapers.

Life in Amin's Uganda fluctuated from the dreadful to the ridiculous. Amin wanted color television so Uganda spent millions of dollars for new television broadcasting equipment, but the only color television sets in the country were in the departure lounge at Entebbe Airport. Kampala streets were renamed; January 25th Avenue, Economic War Boulevard, etc. Murchison Falls became Kabalega Falls and Queen Elizabeth National Park became Ruwenzori National Park. In July of 1973, Lake Edward was renamed Lake Idi Amin Dada. Not many people really disapproved of africanizing the name, but most doubted Amin's true motives. All Mohammed Ali fights were beamed into

Uganda live by satellite. When Ali won, Amin said this proved the power of Allah and the superiority of Islam as a religion.

Members of military were always being given medals. Several hundred were handed out at each ceremony. Amin awarded himself so many medals that they covered the entire left side of his uniform coat from shoulder to hem. All of these honors, of course, were "given" to him by his loyal troops.

Amin made his pilgrimage to Mecca and so could be called Al Haji. Later he was promoted to Field Marshal and finally in June 1976 was "forced" to accept the title of President for Life due to the demands of the people. Thus his official title was His Excellency, Al Haji, Field Marshal, Dr. Idi Amin Dada. V.C. (Victory Cross), D.S.O. (Distinguished Service Order), M.C. (Military Cross), Life President of the Republic of Uganda and Commander and Chief of the Armed Forces.

Dealing with Amin was a diplomat's nightmare. Foreign ambassadors never knew what to expect. Initially Amin was a friend of all western countries including Israel. During his first year in power he visited Britain and the Vatican. In fact, Britain was the first non-African nation to recognize Amin's regime. In February, 1972, Amin visited

140

Muhmmar Ghadaffi in Libya and issued a joint communiqué condemning Israel. Within a month, the Israelis were given seventy two hours to leave Uganda. The Israelis complied but managed to disable most of their construction equipment that remained. Amin then shifted his alliance to the Arab world. Libyan and Egyptian personnel and money poured into Uganda. Uganda's foreign policy was anti-Zionist, anti-Israeli, anti-Colonialist, anti-Christian, pro-Arab, pro-Palestinian, pro-Russian, and pro-Islam.

Amin regularly taunted and baited his "enemies". He sent Richard Nixon a telegram wishing him a quick recovery from Watergate. He started a "Save Britain" fund to send food to unemployed Britons. He encouraged the Scots, Irish and Welsh to wage a war of independence against Britain. He asked for bodyguards to be sent from Britain to accompany him to Princess Anne's wedding. (He was never invited to attend.) He proposed building a monument to honor Hitler, a project he eventually discarded.

Amin's relations with other African countries were not much better. He constantly attacked President Nyerere of Tanzania for giving asylum to Milton Obote. However, at one point, Amin said he loved Nyerere and if Nyerere had been a woman, Amin would have married him, even though Nyerere had a lot of gray hair. Hours and hours of Amin's inane ramblings filled the air waves and newspapers.

In 1973, Lake Albert in western Uganda was renamed Lake Mobutu Sese Seko in honor of the President of Zaire. This was to cement the long-standing good relations between the two countries. In 1975, Amin broke diplomatic relations with Zaire. Uganda-Kenya relations were almost comical. When Uganda's economy collapsed, the only thing that kept Uganda afloat was its proximity to Kenya. In October, 1972, I began working with the East African Community. This was a common market type arrangement between Kenya, Uganda and Tanzania. Certain services, i.e. post office, railways and harbors, customs and the East African Literature Bureau that published and sold books, were jointly owned and operated by the three countries. The revenues from these services were used to support research institutions. The freshwater fisheries research facility was where I worked. The other research institutions covered a wide range of endeavors from marine fisheries to virus research to forestry research.

A council of ministers and a legislature governed the Community. The ruling body, the Community

142

Authority, was comprised of the heads of state of the three countries. The research organizations and office of other Community components were located in all three countries. As an employee of the Community, you could be sent to work in any of the three countries, so Ugandans worked in Kenya, Tanzanians in Uganda etc. This meant a great deal of travel back and forth across the borders. Employees of the Community usually got preferential treatment at the borders. They all carried Community identification cards and Interstate Passes that gave them a certain amount of prestige. The number of whites who held positions in the Community was very small. Most were on short term contracts as experts in a specific field. East Africans efficiently ran the Community. It was so well run and profitable, that Zambia and Somalia expressed serious interest in joining. The Community had its share of corruption and bad management, but it thrived and prospered. It was held up as a shining example of economic cooperation to the rest of Africa.

Once Amin came to power, it was amazing that the Community stayed intact as long as it did. There had always been idealistic differences between the free enterprise of Jomo Kenyatta and the African socialism of Julius Nyerere. President Obote had provided a balance between the two. But when you add the unpredictability of Idi Amin, any hope of success faded. At the Kenya-Uganda border, Kenya money could be purchased at 5 to 1 rate, that is 500 shillings Uganda for 100 shillings Kenya when, theoretically, the currencies of the three countries were at parity. These transactions were conducted openly even though they were illegal.

Initially, Kenya did not seem to mind. There was a great demand for her goods and her economy benefited from Uganda's troubles. Businessmen would buy goods in Kenya and sell them in Uganda for seven or eight times the price. All those items that Uganda still produced, like coffee, were smuggled to Kenya and sold for Kenya currency.

For a farmer to sell his coffee in Uganda was foolish. In James' home district of Bugisu, some of the best coffee in the world is grown. The Bugisu Cooperative would buy all the coffee from the farmers, pay them well and then sell the coffee to the government. But now the co-op had no money and even if they did, there was nothing to buy with Uganda money. Although the risks of taking coffee into Kenya were great, the rewards were well worth it. The army patrolled the border to apprehend the coffee smugglers whom they often killed and then sold the coffee

144

and kept the profits.

I worked for the East African Freshwater Fisheries Research Organization (EAFFRO). It was headquartered in Jinja but there were sub-stations in Kisumu, Kenya and Mwanza, Tanzania. At fairly regular intervals, I had to travel, more to Kenya than to Tanzania. My travel allowances were paid in Kenya currency that allowed me to buy the necessities we lacked and pray that I could get them back across the border. Whenever I crossed the border from Kenya to Uganda, I never knew how the Uganda border guards would react. Sometimes the searches were cursory, sometimes they were exhaustive. It did not matter if you flew or came by bus or taxi or Community vehicle. The uncertainties were the same.

On one occasion, I crossed on a bus. I had sugar, salt, and some children's clothes. The solider on duty was drunk. He asked me why I had so much sugar (10 lbs.). I replied it was for my children. He accused me of being a smuggler, pointed his rifle at my chest and threatened to shoot. Other passengers tried to speak up for me but he was adamant. I tried to remain calm as my mind raced. There had been numerous cases of people being detained at the border and then raped or robbed or worse. I knew that I had to act before the bus left and I knew that Uganda soldiers liked money and trinkets. I profusely apologized for violating the law and asked the solider if I could make up for my mistake by offering him some Kenya money and half of the sugar. He lowered the gun and accepted the money and sugar. He still seemed reluctant to let me go. I remembered that I had bought some cigarillos for James. The solider smiled broadly as he lit up one of the small cigars and told me that I could go.

Usually, at least one of the soldiers at the border could read, and speak English. If they looked at my Uganda passport and noticed that my birthplace was the United States, the inevitable question was "Do you know Mohammed Ali?" My reply could be "No, but we come from the same home town." Or my reply could be "Oh, yes. We went to school together and our families are very close." The degree of my exaggeration depended on what goods I was carrying and the level of hostility of the border guards; whatever worked.

EAFFRO had a trawler named the Ibis that had been given to the Community by the United Nations. The boat trawled in different parts Lake Victoria to study fish populations, feeding and breeding habits. The Ibis would often return with several tons of fish. The scientist would remove the fish they wanted to study and the rest were left to be distributed among the staff. On several occasions, the contents of the fish were gruesome reminders of Amin's atrocities. We found a human eye in one small fish, a finger in another. In a Nile Perch which is a rather large fish, we found a human forearm with a watch still ticking. The army often came and searched the ship and accused us of smuggling and being guerrillas. Eventually, using the boat in Uganda became too dangerous and it only sailed in Kenyan and Tanzanian waters.

By 1973 relations with Kenya began to deteriorate when the number of refugees fleeing Amin's tyranny became burdensome. Ugandans were taking jobs that Kenyans felt they should have. Mafuta Mingis with access to Kenya money flaunted their wealth with wild, raucous behavior in Kenyan cities. But the biggest barrier to good relations was Amin's rhetoric.

At one point he claimed that the Rift Valley should be the natural border between Kenya and Uganda. So he claimed all the territory west of the Rift Valley for Uganda. This infuriated the Kenyans who broadcast an entire Sunday afternoon of radio programs telling Amin exactly what would happen if he dared to cross the border. There were expulsions of Kenyans from Uganda, expulsions of Ugandans from Kenya and Tanzania. Amin even mounted an invasion of Tanzania in an irrational attempt to carve a pathway to the sea. It was a brief but bloody border war. Uganda lost.

Amin's only friends were the Arabs. They sent money, troops, guns whatever he wanted. Palestinians were offered a homeland in western Uganda and Ugandans were urged to volunteer and fight against Israel. The Egyptians and Libyans who came to Uganda were not well liked. They were arrogant and had a condescending attitude towards Africans and especially African women. On one occasion I saw and Arab expert thrown out of a window because he insulted a man's wife at a dance. Fortunately, he landed on a bush and was not seriously hurt.

Of course not all Arabs or all Libyans or all Egyptians are prejudiced. In fact, most Muslims were appalled at what Amin did in the name of Islam. But, in general, the representatives sent to Amin's Uganda as business advisors and experts did not make a good impression.

Soviet-Uganda relations were also mercurial. The Soviet Union was proclaimed to be Uganda's best friend. For one year, Russian arms and Russian doctors appeared throughout the nation. Uganda military personnel were sent to the Soviet Union for training. But the honeymoon was short and that relationship, like all others, except the Arab connection, soon soured. Amin expelled the Russians and them decided to let them stay. The Soviet presence, however, was never the same again.

One of the most embarrassing incidents perpetrated by Amin involved Princess Elizabeth of Toro or Elizabeth Bagaya as she was know in Europe and the United States. Amin appointed her Uganda's ambassador to the United Nations. She is an intelligent, beautiful woman and despite being given the almost hopeless assignment of representing Amin's Uganda, Elizabeth Bagaya did a credible job. Many people wondered why she accepted the position. She could have just run away as those before her had. Ms Bagaya has said that she accepted the position because she loved her country and thought that she could help. As a well know member of a Ugandan royal family, she hoped to salvage Uganda's image.

In November of 1974, Elizabeth Bagaya was recalled to Uganda from New York. She was immediately dismissed from her position by Amin who accused her of having sexual intercourse with an unidentified European in a toilet at Orly Airport in Paris on her way home. The charges were ridiculous. Ms. Bagaya was surrounded with reporters from the time she entered the airport until she left.

Further, such behavior for a woman of her breeding and background was most unlikely. She had been a model in Europe for years and radiated poise and sophistication. Everyone was stupefied.

But Amin was not through yet. On the front page of the Voice of Uganda, Amin printed a nude, full length profile allegedly of Ms. Bagaya to attest to her low moral character. To even the untrained eye it was apparent that Ms. Bagaya's head had been put on a picture of someone else's body. The skin shades of the head and body in the picture were clearly different. Everyone feared for Ms Bagaya's safety when she was not seen for almost one week. Amin said she was under house arrest. He finally allowed her to be photographed to prove she was still alive. She was eventually released and wisely, left Uganda. The Bagaya affair was the ultimate humiliation. Ugandans are proud people, proud of themselves, and proud of their country. To have their president, albeit not their chose leader, humiliate and muddy Uganda's name all over the world was devastating.

Uganda is a predominantly Christian country. Only 15% of the people are Muslim. Before the coup, all religions got along well there were no conflicts. But Amin attempted to destroy Christianity in Uganda. He persecuted

150

Christians, belittled their beliefs and eventually had the highest ranking church official killed.

When the Uganda Martyrs Shrine was opened, Amin arrived in full Arab regalia, robes, burnoose and all, and muttered words in Arabic before cutting the ribbon. Amin subsequently tried to build a shrine to Muslim Uganda martyrs whom no one seemed to know about. But every time the shrine was started, it was mysteriously dismantled during the night. He soon abandoned the project. Muslims gradually but surely moved into key government positions and were given preferential treatment on all fronts. On Islamic holidays milk, meat, sugar, rice were all readily available. On Christian holidays the cupboard was bare. On Christmas and Easter, Uganda Television showed Muslim dances from Saudi Arabia all day long. When Catholic Archbishop Nsubuga was made a Cardinal, his return from Rome was an occasion for great celebration. He was greeted by large crowds at Entebbe Airport. Well wishers lined the road all the way into Kampala. Amin was livid. He issued an order that no public gatherings or parades could be held for anyone but him. He accused the well wishers of blocking the road and obstructing military traffic. After all becoming a Prince of the Catholic church certainly could not be considered cause for celebration.

Rev. John Wasikye, the man who married us and christened our children, was on his way to a meeting in Kampala when he was arrested. Rev. Wasikye was a brave, outspoken critic of the government. His sermons pleaded with Ugandans to keep their faith and stand on the promise of the cross. He was never seen again.

By trying to make Uganda a Muslim country, Amin hoped to win Arab support and dollars. If the Arab world believed it had a foothold in East Africa, Amin thought they would back him to the hilt. The people who were mainly targeted during the Islamization of Uganda were women. Amin's government imposed restriction after restriction on women. It became essential to listen to the news everyday in Uganda. The 5 p.m. and 8 p.m. news broadcasts were the ones where the government spokesman usually announced major policy changes or new rules. Soon after the visit of the late King Faisal of Saudi Arabia to Uganda, Amin imposed a dress code for women. No dress could be more than three inches above the knee. No splits or slits in dresses were allowed. Further, the wearing of wigs and use of makeup was banned. Amin said that wigs were made from the hair of dead Europeans and this was making females forget how to behave like African

152

women. Also women could not wear pants. The only exceptions were women in the police force and prison service.

The announcement of the new dress code was made on a 5 p.m. radio newscast. For those women at work or away from home who were in violation of the new rules, a rude awakening was in store. The army and military police arrested thousands of women, many of whom were beaten, raped and humiliated. Some had their heads shaved or were made to stand or squat for hours or hop like frogs.

The enforcement of the new rules was as haphazard as everything else. One major problem stemmed from confusion about where the knee starts. Some measured from the top of the knee joint, some from the bottom of the knee joint, some from where the knee bends. Finally, in desperation and for their own safety, women only wore long skirts and dresses. These clothes were called Amin Nvako, which means Amin leave me alone. Again, in typical Amin style, part of the order was rescinded. When Pakistani experts came to Uganda, their wives wore pants as part of their national dress. So pants were once again allowed for women.

Despite Amin's thinly veiled persecution,

Christianity flourished. Every Sunday the churches were full. Although many said that God had forgotten Uganda, faith was what kept most of us going. Many Muslims did not agree with Amin and said that what he was doing violated the basic principles of Islam.

In 1977, the Archbishop of the Church of Uganda, was an unassuming man named Jowann Luwum. He was a Langi, a danger in itself in Amin's Uganda. Archbishop Luwum was also a man of principle and faith. He watched Amin's atrocities as long as he could. Finally, in an incredible act of faith and bravery, he along with several other clergymen signed a letter addressed to Amin. It protested the acts of violence and torture and pleaded for sanity and reason. Amin received the letter and thanked the Archbishop for his concern. The two were photographed together and Amin of course denied that his government or army had anything to do with the murders. On February 17, 1977 Archbishop Luwum was arrested along with two of Amin's long time cabinet members. They were all killed in an "auto accident." All of the bodies were bullet ridden and it was reported that the victims' hands were handcuffed behind their backs. The official story was that the "prisoners" were killed in an escape attempt that caused the "auto accident". An international commission sent to investigate the deaths was banned from Uganda.

Amin's personal life was national news in Uganda.
Accounts of his marriages, divorces, births of his children
were recounted in detail by the media. In 1971 when Amin
seized power, he had three wives, Malyamu, Kay and Nora.
As a Muslim he could have four wives. Malyamu Kibedi
was the elder wife. Her brother was made Minister of
Foreign Affairs. Kay Adroa married Amin in 1966. She
was from West Nile and had been educated at Makerere.
Nora Amin was a Langi. She was never in the public eye
much and appeared quite young and innocent.

On September 24, 1972 Amin married his fourth
wife, Medina. She was a dancer with group called the
Heartbeat of Africa. Amin reportedly did not inform his
current wives of his plans. The first they heard of it was on
the evening news.

Uganda was run on rumor and speculation. Some
things could be confirmed through foreign newscasts or if
the story came from a reliable insider. But you never quite
knew what was true and what was rumor. So many horrible
stories were finally confirmed by personal experience or
indisputable reports, that when you were told anything
about Amin you could easily believe it was true. For
instance, Amin's children. He had about thirty children by

his wives and other women. I recall a set of twins that were allegedly born on Christmas Day. It was said that they were born earlier but Amin chose Christmas as the birthday to make the event more important. Even Amin's birthday kept changing and eventually settled on New Years Day. His place of birth changed according to where he was at the time. Wherever he gave a speech that was the place he was born or grew up.

Wherever Amin went he took one or more of his children, especially when he went abroad. Usually he took his sons. His favorite was Moses. Moses even wore a replica of his father's uniform down to a chest full of miniature medals. Reportedly, Amin and members of his tribe believed in witchcraft. He was told by a witch doctor that his children were his magic. As long as he had his children with him he could not be hurt. His children were almost never photographed wearing short sleeves. They were said to wear numerous amulets to protect them and their father from evil spirits or whatever. It was widely believed that in the fading days of his regime, Amin sacrificed his favorite son Moses to the spirits, believing that such an act would insure immortality and invincibility.

In March 1974 Amin divorced Kay, Nora and Malyamu. He gave ridiculous reasons for his actions. The one that I remember most clearly was that Kay was his cousin and too closely related to be married to him. They had been married for almost eight years and had several children. In April, Malyamu was arrested for allegedly being involved in black market activity. She was released but soon afterwards suffered serious injuries in a automobile "accident" with a military vehicle. While she was in the hospital, Amin visited her and said that "women who disobeyed their husbands" always met with misfortune. Malyamu eventually managed to get out of Uganda.

Kay Adroa Amin was not as lucky. What happened to her was barbaric and tragic. Her dismembered body was found in gunny sacks in the trunk of a car belonging to a doctor who had allegedly performed an abortion on Kay a few days before. Here is where the story gets muddled. Either there were complications after the abortion, Kay hemorrhaged and died and the doctor panicked, dismembered her body and hoped to dispose of it somehow, or Amin found out about the abortion and vented his anger on his ex-wife. Whatever the truth, a lovely, intelligent woman met a tragic death. I never heard what happened to Nora.

The impact of Aminism on our family was

predictable. Our quiet lifestyle was plunged into disarray and disorder. Things we had taken for granted were suddenly difficult or impossible to obtain. Services whose existence we had ignored were unavailable. A country we loved and cherished became a place of terror and death.

Through my job at the fisheries, I was allocated a house on a hill at one end of Jinja overlooking the lake. At least once a week, I walked to the other end of town (about three miles) to buy food at the open market. As I walked I remembered the old Jinja. Shops filled with yard goods, food, toiletries, people standing, talking, restaurants and food shops filling the air with international aromas. I remembered the post office with its first day covers and express overseas telegrams, the open market with piles of tomatoes, groundnuts, cabbages, bread, butter, milk, soap, salt, sugar. But in the Uganda of 1975, the scenario had been altered considerably. The post office sometimes had no stamps. All letters were read and stamped "Approved by the President's Office" before they were sent abroad or delivered internally. The shops were almost empty. You could buy $100 bottle of brandy but not soap. The restaurants served only bread and tea usually without sugar. Crowds jostled for a place in line to get a taxi, get on a bus, buy a pound of salt. The market stalls were sparsely

stocked, the piles were smaller, the prices tripled. There
was always the threat of raids by the military police who
would sweep down on the market, beat up the sellers
accusing them of black marketeering and harass anyone
else who was around. The young men who used to carry
your purchase the length of the town in their wheelbarrows
now demanded twenty times the price. There was no toilet
paper, no flour, no hope, no relief.

As an American, being in this situation stirred many
emotions and feelings for me. Most of all it made me not
just homesick but grateful for my native country and its
freedoms. I sometimes felt like a voyeur secretly observing
some absurd, horrific movie. How could human beings be
so ruthless? How could these ignorant butchers rule a
country filled with warm, caring people? Uganda had
produced some of the most educated men and women in
Africa. It had been ruled and shaped by one of the greatest
nations in the world. How had this happened?

Pictures flashed in my mind of the Freedom Riders
and marchers being beaten in the civil rights struggle. I
thought of the three young civil rights workers found slain
in Mississippi and the many other bodies of unidentified
black men found during the search. I recalled scenes of the
near riot conditions at the 1968 convention in Chicago,

reports of urban crime, political corruption, legislative gridlock. America certainly had its problems, but somehow, some way it always seemed to work out. The original aims of the United States Constitution always managed to prevail, sometimes after years of abuse or injustice, even death, but democratic principles survived. Leaders were sometimes assassinated, those who spoke out were often targeted or persecuted, but the right to oppose, to challenge, to even defy those is power was always protected.

During Watergate, my students would ask what all the fuss was about. What had President Nixon done? I talked about betrayal of public trust, misuse of authority, illegal entry, burglary, and conduct unbecoming the President of the United States. One student asked, "How many people did he kill?" None. "How much money did he take from the treasury and hide in other countries?" None. "Why didn't he order the army to take over control of the government instead of resigning?" That required more of an answer than I could muster on the spur of the moment. They were all amazed that the people of country acting through their elected representatives, could force the president of a country to resign, without firing a shot. Life, liberty and the Bill of Rights took on a very different meaning. Walter Winchell said, "Too many people expect wonders from democracy, when the most wonderful thing of all is just having it."

Chapter 8
Meeting, Book and Airplane

1975 and 1976 were to be Amin's years of worldwide attention and infamy. He would catapult himself and Uganda into the consciousness of the world with a book, a meeting and an airplane.

Dennis Hills, a Briton, wrote a book about Uganda called *The White Pumpkin*. Mr. Hills was still in Uganda when the book was published and Amin took offense at some of Mr. Hills' observations in the book. What the "offensive" statements were is unimportant. The point was that Amin directed his anger at Dennis Hill's. Amin insulted and belittled Hills publicly, then finally arrested him in April, 1975. Two months later Hills was sentenced to death. Britain and the world were outraged. Pleas for mercy, clemency and compassion poured in from all over the world.

President Nyerere of Tanzania made a very important and appropriate observation at the height of the Hills affair. He observed that hundreds of thousands of Ugandans had died or "disappeared" since 1971 but some countries had not protested or petitioned Amin for mercy.

However, when one *white* man was threatened, the world's nations, including black ruled African countries, cried out for clemency. The British government used ever diplomatic tool at its disposal while dealing with an unstable, volatile, unpredictable, megalomaniac. They sent letters, envoys and eventually their Foreign Minister.

In Uganda, everyone was acutely aware of the seriousness of the situation. If Amin executed Hills, the British government would retaliate, perhaps backed by their allies. Many hoped Hills would be executed so that Britain or someone would have an excuse to intervene and perhaps topple Amin. On July 10, 1975 the British Foreign Minister, James Callaghan, arrived in Uganda and left the next day with Dennis Hills. It was almost as if Amin felt he had made the British bend to his will.

One factor that mitigated heavily on Amin's decision to release Hills was the Organization of African Unity (OAU) summit meeting. The summit was to begin in Kampala on July 28, 1975. Amin knew that many heads of state would be reluctant to attend if he was still holding Hills or if he executed him.

Elaborate preparations were made for the conference. There was already a beautiful conference center in Kampala. However, with the country in a state of economic chaos, staging a meeting for heads of state was a risky proposition, but Amin proved equal to the task. He used precious foreign exchange to buy Fiats, Mercedes, and a fleet of vans. In total over 300 cars were purchased. The luxury hotels, bare for months, were stocked with food and drink. However, the goodies were reserved for OAU guests, not Ugandans. One vacant store on the main street in Kampala was filled with sugar, salt, cooking oil, flour, all the things unavailable to the public. It was surrounded with armed guards twenty four hours a day.

Ugandans from six to sixty were brought into Kampala in every available conveyance to line the street and cheer for the visitors. They were rehearsed in how to clap, how to wave, given appropriate signs to hold, and flowers to throw. To refuse to go meant death. Amin was a smiling, jovial host who greeted his guests warmly and only allowed them to see what he wanted them to see. There were a few embarrassing incidents for Amin during the conference. Several explosive charges were set off at various locations around the city. Leaflets were covertly distributed around Kampala telling of the murder and torture perpetrated by Amin's government. All of this was blamed, of course, on guerrillas from Tanzania.

It was the custom that the president of host country

be elected Africa's spokesman for the next year. So in July 1975, Al Haji, Field Marshall, Dr. Idi Amin Dada V.C., D.S.O., M.C. became Chairman of the Organization of African Unity.

At the end of the meeting, many of the cars purchased for the conference were stolen and driven to Kenya and sold by army personnel, civilians, anyone who could get them. The goods displayed in the shops disappeared also. To celebrate the end of the O.A.U. conference, Amin got married again. At that time he only had one wife, Medina. His new bride Sarah had been a singer with one of the army bands. The wedding was a spectacle. They were married at the conference center. All diplomats were required to attend. Amin was decked out in his uniform with medals from shoulder to knee and belly button to armpit. The father of the bride, with quivering voice, told everyone how happy and honored he was for his daughter to marry the president. You could see the fear in his eyes. The bride was neither blushing nor radiant. A Muslim priest, using the Koran performed the ceremony. However, the wording of the ceremony was the traditional Christian vows. It was an insult to both religions and some Arab diplomats walked out.

After the formal ceremony the bride and groom

walked under an arch of swords into the garden. There they sat, several hundred feet from their guests, surrounded by bodyguards. Traditional dancers entertained the newlyweds but were not allowed to get too close.

October 1975 saw Amin visiting the United Nations to address the General Assembly. The Ugandan ambassador to the UN read Amin's speech. Everyone was relieved that the "Jungle Marshall" had not said a word, but the celebration was premature. Amin rose and addressed the General Assembly in broken Luganda, a language for which there was no translator. He then spoke in English, rambling on and on aimlessly. Uganda in particular, and Africa as a whole were embarrassed and humiliated.

But soon Amin was to be the one embarrassed and humiliated in one of the most daring military operations ever executed. It all began on June 27, 1976. Air France Flight 139 originated in Tel Aviv. It stopped in Athens and then took off for Paris. It never arrived. Soon after leaving Athens, the plane and its 258 passengers were hijacked. Terrorists with guns and explosives diverted the plane to Benghazi where it refueled. Then they flew to Uganda and landed at Entebbe Airport on Monday June 28, 1976. We in Uganda thought that the plane had landed to refuel and then would be on its way. When we learned that most of the passengers were Israelis and that the hijackers were sympathetic to the PLO, we knew there would be trouble.

There were really two airports at Entebbe. The old airport built by the Israelis ,that was no longer in use, and the new airport built by the Yugoslavs. The plane was at the old airport with the passengers still aboard. Entebbe was completely sealed off and only authorized military personnel could get within ten miles of the airport. Every radio in Uganda was tuned to the BBC or Voice of America or some outside news source. Radio Uganda reported that Amin was in touch with the hijackers, the plane was surrounded by Ugandan troops and the situation was under control.

We heard that Amin was in touch with the Israeli government and negotiations were in progress. We also learned that the hijackers were demanding the release of fifty-three alleged terrorists in prison in Israel, West Germany, France, Switzerland and Kenya, demands that Amin called "very reasonable". However, in Uganda, it was still unclear what Amin's role was in the drama. Was he peacemaker, instigator, glory seeker or of all of the above? Had he planned for the plane to come to Uganda? Was he going to add his own demands to the hijackers?

Despite Amin's anti-Israeli posture and close ties

167

with the Arabs, Israel was well respected in Uganda. Her success in defending herself against unfriendly neighbors, daring military tactics and fierce loyalty of her citizens was admired. When Dennis Hills was under threat of death, Ugandans thought that Britain would act. But if Israeli passengers were harmed, Ugandans <u>knew</u> that Israel would retaliate.

Field Marshall Amin was in his glory. He persuaded the hijackers to allow the passengers to leave the plane and enter the old abandoned air terminal. He greeted the hostages, smiling and wearing a cowboy hat. He said he would make their stay as pleasant as possible. He visited on another occasion in full dress uniform with all his decorations, accompanied by his son Moses who wore a replica of his father's outfit down to the miniature medals.

On Wednesday, June 30, forty seven hostages were allowed to leave. On Thursday, July 1, more hostages were released leaving ninety-three hostages who were Israeli, Jewish or had Jewish sounding names. One passenger, Mrs. Dorah Block, had been taken to a local hospital when she choked on food. The negotiations continued, but as night fell on Uganda, Saturday July 3, 1976 the situation was critical. The hijackers' deadline was early the next morning.

I awoke early that Sunday. It was the American

Bicentennial Anniversary. July 4, 1976. I wondered what my parents were doing. I wondered where James was. He had gone to Butta earlier in the week. Maybe he was waiting to see what would happen at Entebbe before he tried to come back. I turned to radio Uganda. It was playing only martial music. I switched to the BBC and could not believe what I heard. In the early hours of Sunday morning, the Israelis had raided Entebbe, rescued the hostages and killed the hijackers. Amin and his army had been caught flat-footed.

The Israelis distracted the Uganda army with explosive charges set off at the new airport. The lights were disconnected and Amin's "crack troops" ran. Those that remained, shot at each other until the daylight revealed that the enemy was long gone. Amin was furious. His army had been humiliated and he had been made a fool of. The old airport, some of his military jets, the runways at the new airport were in shambles. He berated his army. Had he not bought them sophisticated military equipment only to have them let the Israelis walk in untouched? Were they not the best army in Africa? Was he not the greatest military tactician in the world? What could have gone wrong? The personnel on duty in the tower at Entebbe that night were reportedly executed on Amin's orders. All military

169

personnel were put on twenty-four hour alert and confined
to the barracks. Amin claimed he lost only twenty soldiers
but the day after the raid, several truckloads of caskets
passed through Jinja. All the soldiers killed were buried in
a mass grave nearby.

Ugandans were ecstatic. Amin and his thugs had
been shown up for what they were. For the first time since
the coup, army vehicles and troops were openly jeered and
heckled. People laughed at them and taunted them saying,
"If you don't behave, we'll call back the Israelis!!" James
told me that when the news of the raid reached the villages,
people shouted, "The children of God have come to save
us!"

The commander of the Israeli rescue force was
killed during the raid. Mrs. Dorah Block was taken from
the hospital by unidentified men and never seen again.

Chapter 9

Leaving Home, Going Home

I was not quite sure what awakened me that night.
Perhaps the sound of tires on the gravel in the driveway, or
maybe some sixth sense that danger might be near.

I lay very still for a moment straining to hear. The
familiar sounds of the East African night filled the room,
the rhythmic chirping of insects, the mournful wail of night
birds, the soft rustle of fronds of the banana trees stirred by
the gentle night breeze. But there was another sound, the
quiet, steady hum of a car engine.

I slid out of bed and crawled along next to the wall
until I was under the open window. Slowly raising my
head, I chanced a look outside. The moon shown brightly in
the clear East African sky and I could clearly see the Land
Rover in the driveway. Three men sat inside talking.

Who were they? Were they state research officers or
military intelligence or whatever Idi Amin's thugs called
themselves? Had they come for my husband James? He
was out of town. Maybe that was a good thing. Maybe they
would just leave. Or would they take me instead? Our two
children were asleep in their room. They usually did not

hurt children, but that gave me little comfort.

There was a cool breeze blowing in through the window but my body was covered with a thin coating of perspiration. I wiped my clammy hands on my thighs and reached out once more with trembling hands to ease back the curtains. The twisting, paved road and gravel driveway leading up to the cluster of three houses where we lived were bathed in moonlight. Opposite the houses there was a steep descending slope covered with brush. Our house and the single houses on either side sat far above the city and were fairly isolated. Suddenly the Land Rover door opened and two of the men stepped out and began to walk towards the path at the back of the house. They were too for away for me to see their faces or determine if they were armed.

Gently easing the curtain back into place, I crept along the wall to the bedroom door. Bent double, I crossed the dining room and the kitchen being careful not to be seen through the kitchen windows. With infinite care, I opened the door to the service porch and prayed that what I wanted was still there. I paused momentarily to let my eyes adjust to the new darkness. I searched for the broad blade machete-like panga. It was so close that I almost missed it. I grasped the wooden handle. Its weight and size gave me some comfort.

I moved stealthily to the back door at the rear of the service porch and stood in the corner behind the door with the panga raised above my head. I could hear the men walking down the path, talking softly. I closed my eyes waiting for the knock, the shouted command to open up, the splintering of wood as the door was kicked in. "Please God, take care of my babies." My heart pounded so loudly, surely they too could hear. The footsteps came closer and closer and then.... continued along the path. They had passed by. I lowered the panga but still held it in front of me with both hands. I moved cautiously to the right and risked a look out of the back window. The two men walked along the path with their heads lowered and their hands in their pockets. They reached the house next door and one of them looked back over his shoulder. Even with the moonlight it was too dark for me to see their faces. They were not in uniform and I could not see any weapons, but that did not mean much. Terror came in many disguises. Reinforcements could be on the way. I could still faintly hear the engine of the Land Rover, running as it stood in the driveway waiting.

One man raised his hand and pounded on the back door. No reply. He knocked again. No answer. The men retraced their steps along the path. They had realized their mistake and were coming back to our house. I grasped the handle of the panga more firmly and leapt to my position behind the door. But the men walked down between the two houses and turned toward my neighbor's front door. They stepped onto the front porch and knocked again. Suddenly the outside light shattered the darkness. The two men stepped forward and were clearly visible. It was my neighbor's brother and nephew. As they entered the house, the Land Rover backed out and sped away. All was dark and silent once more.

I was sweating profusely as I stumbled back towards the bedroom. I looked in on the children who were still sleeping peacefully. I collapsed onto the bed and began to shiver. The tears of relief and fear and anger began to flow. Why did we have to live like this? I did not know how much more I could take. "Please God help us to get out. Don't let us die here. Please God help us!" Those words resounded thorough my mind. They were with me twenty four hours a day, if not consciously then just below the surface like a haunting refrain I could not forget.

I dozed fitfully until 7 am I knew the time because the sun was creeping over the horizon. The time of sunrise and sunset never varied by more that twenty minutes so close to the equator. At least some things never changed. I could hear the muffled sounds of Edward and Lillian babbling away in three different languages as the nanny gave them their breakfast. As I stood in the bathroom preparing to go to work, I thought about James. He had gone to the village to help his mother, I hoped he would be back that day. This was all so difficult for him. I knew how much it hurt to see his homeland desecrated. He seemed to blame himself for putting the children and me in danger, but it was not his fault. There was nothing anyone could do but try and cope.

Mechanically, I began my morning routine. We were low on toothpaste and soap. That meant someone would have to go to Kenya soon. How ridiculous, a 200 mile trip to buy toothpaste and sugar and salt and almost everything else. I remembered when a trip to Bungoma was at treat, when there was no scrambling for buses, no guns at the border, no black market money exchange. Some things had changed a great deal.

After dressing, I stood before the mirror brushing my hair. With my short Afro and cafe au lait complexion I was often mistaken for a Mukiga or Munankole from western Uganda. When I was growing up on the south side of Chicago, I considered my skin color a liability to be overcome. But in East Africa it had allowed me to blend into the background, to be inconspicuous. It had probably saved my life. My mother would hate my hair this way. I knew my parents were worried. I knew they wondered and waited and hoped and prayed the same prayer. "Please God, help them to get out."

The face that stared back from the mirror was very different from that idealistic Peace Corps Volunteer who arrived in Uganda almost ten years earlier. My skin was darkened by the sun. I had lost weight and my dress hung loosely on my five foot four inch frame. The lines of worry and tension around my brown eyes made me look older than my thirty-one years.

I said goodbye to my children. As I stepped outside, the scene that was so threatening the night before, now seemed calm and familiar. From the front of the house, the blue, serene, waters of Lake Victoria were visible over the treetops below, but even the lake was tinged with the blood red color of change. Nothing had escaped. The walk from home to the office was one of the high points of my day. The road was lined with beautiful, fragrant acacia and frangipani trees. Poinsettia bushes with their brilliant red flowers dotted the roadside. There was hibiscus in red and pink and mango trees heavy with ripening fruit. Everyday, I marveled at the outer beauty of Uganda and cringed at the ugliness within.

The sign in front of the building where I worked read East African Freshwater Fisheries Research Organization, East African Community, Jinja, Uganda, East Africa. The building was located about 100 feet from the shores of Lake Victoria. As I entered I exchanged greetings with the other workers. On the wall directly in front of the main entrance was a standard fixture of any East African Community facility, the pictures of the three presidents of the countries that comprised the Community. The picture of the president in whose country the office was located was in the center. So every morning, Amin's picture greeted me; on his left was Julius Nyerere of Tanzania, on his right, Jomo Kenyatta of Kenya. His smile in the photo was friendly and boyish. He looked jovial and innocent. But we who lived under his rule since knew better. We knew about the death, pillage, rape, confusion, destruction, but most of all the immobilizing, pervasive fear. It was with you all the time, like a cloak around your shoulders you could not remove. It filled every waking hour and made you jump at every shadow, every noise in the night. "Please God......"

"Hey you!" a harsh male voice barked out in Swahili from behind me. I spun around and he was standing in the doorway. The sunlight was shining in behind him so for a few seconds, I was temporarily blinded. The first things I could distinguish clearly were his black knee high laced boots. The khaki uniform pants were tucked into the boots and the belt around his waist held a holstered pistol and a sheathed knife. A machine gun hung from his left shoulder by a frayed strap. The insignia on his olive drab shirt told me he was an army sergeant. He was wearing a red beret that made his very dark, black skin seem almost bluish purple. The long straight tribal marks in the flesh over his cheekbones told me he was from West Nile Province. He was one of Amin's people. He took me so much by surprise that I almost answered him in English. Many members of the army did not speak English and they viewed its use as a mark of arrogance or a flaunting of your education. Many had paid with their lives for speaking English at the wrong time.

I mumbled a greeting in Swahili without my voice trembling too much. "Wapi Mukubwa?" he bellowed. My heart sank. He wanted to see the director of the facility. I was fairly sure that he was not there but my mind raced through possible replies I could give. Had he come to arrest the director, to kill him, to make him disappear as so many had since Amin "liberated" Uganda?

I told him that the director was not in and offered to

help him if I could. He explained what he wanted and I heaved a silent sigh of relief. One of the amphibious tanks Amin bought from Russia was stuck out in the lake and none of the soldiers in it could swim. He needed one of our motorboats to rescue them. I sent him to the chief of the boat crew and then, with a trembling hand, opened the door to my office. I sank into the chair behind the desk.

It is said that every emotion has a flavor. That dry metallic tang in the back of my mouth was the all too familiar taste of terror. My body was covered with thin film of cold perspiration and I could feel the back of my legs sticking to the leather seat of the chair. I could not take much more. I would have to leave soon or go insane. I closed my eyes and my mind repeated those familiar words. "Please God! Help us to get out!" Leaning my head back against the chair, I took deep breaths until my pulse rate returned to normal and my hands were no longer shaking. "Please God help us to get out. Don't let us die here. Please God help us!"

All of the fear, and pressure took their toll on James and me. We did the best we could, but living was difficult. We were frustrated, angry and frightened. We worried too much, drank too much, tried to decide what to do. You might think that the decision to leave was a easy one to

179

make. After all Uganda was in shambles. Going out of the house meant endangering your life. The most basic necessities were almost impossible to get. We had two young children who deserved a chance. Why not just leave? The answer is complex.

Uganda was James' home and he carried most of the responsibility for his family. While we were never able to give much financial help, we did what we could. At the same time we realized that things would not get better in Uganda soon and maybe if we could get out, we would be able to help the family more.

It was a difficult situation for me too. I wanted to fulfill my commitment and obligations to James and his family. I knew I could not take the children and leave James in Uganda. We had to go as a family. I was so terribly homesick and tired of the strain, stress, and fear. At times I felt very exasperated with the Ugandan people. Why not rise up and topple Amin? Why not protest in large numbers? Why did everyone shrug their shoulders and say, "What can you do?" I thought that maybe I did not understand because I was an American. Maybe you had to be born and raised in Africa to understand. I began to feel isolated, just as I had during Peace Corps training. Surely there was something to be done. Maybe if we waited a

180

while Amin would be overthrown and things would improve and the new president would be better. Finally I came to realize that all these feelings stemmed from one irrefutable fact: I had reached the end of my rope. My mind, body and soul were exhausted. I could not take anymore.

Despite all the pressures on our marriage, James and I could always talk. He was frustrated, I was strung out and we often vented our feelings on each other, but we both knew the real target of our anger was the situation we were in. There is a line from the musical *West Side Story* that often came to mind. One of the star-crossed lovers said "There's nothing wrong with us. It's everything around us."

I do not think James and I ever openly admitted that we had to leave. We started talking about going to the States for a "visit". After all, my parents were worried and getting older, at least they should see their grandchildren for a while. And maybe if James got a job we could stay a year or two and then come back when things were better. If I had really been honest with myself, I would have admitted the truth. If I ever got out of Uganda, I would not come back unless things improved greatly and that was unlikely.

James was being torn right down the middle. He

had to choose between his mother and siblings and his wife and children. I understood and sympathized but, I had to leave or lose my mind. Our first serious attempt to leave was in 1975. My family was having a big family reunion in Alabama and we planned to go. But first let me explain about leaving Uganda. It was not a simple matter.

Several factors impinged on Uganda's immigration policy. First, foreign exchange. All airline tickets were paid for in foreign currency so their availability was directly related to Uganda foreign reserve levels. Also, anyone going abroad needed foreign currency for expenses. Second, Amin became increasingly paranoid the longer he stayed in office. He was always looking for imperialist spies and guerrillas. Those returning from abroad or asking to travel abroad were suspect, so to protect himself, he changed the rules on travel on a whim.

The basic procedure for leaving was this. You had to have permission to leave Uganda which was obtained by going to the Ministry of Foreign Affairs or Internal Affairs or Justice or whichever ministry was responsible at that point in time. There you had to justify your reason for wanting to leave. Next you went to the airline and got a statement of the price of a round-trip ticket. You never asked for a one way ticket. You always let them think you were coming back.

Then on to the Bank of Uganda to get permission to buy an airline ticket. This simply means they checked to see if there was enough foreign exchange to buy the ticket. You then had seven days in which to actually purchase the ticket, but first you paid the government a tax of 30% of the total price of the ticket. Then you went back to the Bank of Uganda to ask for foreign currency to use while abroad. Sometimes you got the amount you asked for, sometimes you got nothing.

At some point in this process you were issued a pass. This informed the military commander at Entebbe airport that you were cleared to leave the country. Even if you had a ticket, without the pass you could not leave. The only other alternative was to go to Kenya and buy the airline tickets there, if you had enough Kenya money. However, the Kenya government was understandably reluctant to deplete their foreign exchange to buy plane tickets and give traveling money to Ugandans. The Kenya option was not a viable alternative.

Our biggest problem was where to get the money. We needed almost 40,000 shs (about $6000). We were not Mafuta Mingis but we paid the exorbitant prices for our daily needs. To amass that much money at one time was a

183

problem. James tried every scheme he could think of. He smuggled, he borrowed, he hustled but there was never enough. The summer of 1975 passed and we were no closer to our goal. I dreaded writing and telling my parents we were not coming. I finally did write and said we would try to come at Christmas.

But it was not to be. No matter what we did during the next year, 1976, we could not seem to get the money. My frustration grew, my depression deepened. I stopped writing my parents because I no longer knew what to say. James was gone a great deal of the time, struggling, hustling, trying desperately to get out. He sensed how close I was to the edge. I believe he had also come to grips with the reality that perhaps he could aid his family best by going to the United States, earning money and sending back what he could.

I could not sleep at night. For hours I would be awake listening to the radio. The Voice of America ran old radio programs, Jack Benny, Fibber McGee and Molly, Burns and Allen. I would listen and cry.

Working with the East African Community, I had opportunities to travel to Kenya and Tanzania, sometimes by air, most often by car. I would buy every available foreign magazine and read them several times. I could not bring them back to Uganda with me because of the ban on foreign newspapers, but occasionally I would take a risk and smuggle a Newsweek or Time across the border, especially if there was an article about Uganda. We had to be careful to whom we showed the magazine and burn them page by page when we were through.

I drank very heavily, so did James, so did almost everyone in Uganda. It was a matter of dulling the senses, of forgetting. Escape from reality was the order of the day. I knew it was no good for me, my marriage, or my children. But at that point I was so frustrated and angry and afraid that the only peace I found was in a cloud of alcohol.

It was now early December 1976. I told everyone than I was planning to go to the United States for Christmas. I felt that if I kept saying it, it would come true. James was going to Mbale but before he left we talked. He said he would try and smuggle some coffee to Kenya to make money. I decided to apply for vacation so that I could get my pay in advance. That would help some.

Money was the key. How could I get money? I decided to sell the furniture in the house. Everyone asked why I was selling everything. I told them that we planned to buy all new furniture when we returned. They asked "Are you really coming back?" I assured them that we were. You had to be careful what you said even to those you thought were you friends. Within four days I sold the children's beds, the record player, and most of the dishes. James was returning that day and we were going to move the rest of our belongings to Mbale. We had about a quarter of the money we needed, but we felt that in Mbale we could somehow manage to get the rest. We were operating on pure faith. James sensed my desperation, my obsessive need to leave Uganda.

We rented a small truck and packed up all of our worldly goods. James rode on the back. The children, the driver, and the nanny and I were squeezed into the cab. As the truck pulled away from the house and we left Jinja, I prayed that I would not have to come back in a few weeks. I hoped we would not fail. We could not fail. We just could not fail.

The trip to Mbale was long and tedious. We were stopped at several roadblocks, but it was only the police checking for licenses. We arrived in Mbale and unpacked our things at Patrick's house and then the real battle began. Day after day, James and I went out. We tried to borrow the money. We sold an old car we had. We tried to smuggle in goods from Kenya or smuggle coffee out. On one occasion James had to run from the army. They opened fire on his truck. He abandoned it and ran for his life. We he returned his truck was there, but no coffee.

It was Christmas Eve morning, 1976. I awoke depressed. We had half the needed amount and promises for the rest. I knew I had to call my parents today. They probably thought we were dead. I finally got the overseas operator and the phone was ringing. They were asleep. It was 5 am in Alabama. I wondered what the house looked like. They moved from Chicago to Shorter after I left. Would I ever see them again?

"Hello."

"Mommy?"

"Sara? Where are you? How are you?"

"We're still in Uganda. But we are coming."

When?"

"As soon as we can."

"I've been wondering what happened and if you were alright."

"I know. We were trying to get everything settled before we called."

"Do you have any idea when you'll be here?"

"Hopefully within a few weeks. We'll let you know."

"We're so worried and we pray for you everyday."

"Keep praying and we <u>will</u> be home."

187

My hand was trembling as I put down the phone. The tears burned behind my eyes. But I could not cry. If I started I would not be able to stop.

Within one week we finally have enough money. I do not know where it all came from, some borrowed, some given, most from Divine Intervention. At that point I did not care.

The taxi ride to Kampala was cramped and hectic. We arose at dawn to go the taxi park. James bribed a driver to give us seats. At Jinja we waited three hours for a taxi to Kampala. All along I clutched my handbag with more than 40,000 shs in it. It was our lives that I carried.

Our first stop was the Ministry of Internal Affairs where the Permanent Secretary must give us permission to leave Uganda. I had a letter from my employer saying that I was on annual leave and wished to visit the United States. I had my own personal statement saying that my father was very ill and that he wanted to see his grandchildren. The Permanent Secretary knew James' father and greeted us warmly. He asked a few questions and signed the exit permit. He gave us a pass to use at the airport. It was good for two weeks. Next we went to the Air France office. They computed the cost of round trip tickets for the four of us. It was over 30,000 shs ($4300). On to the Ministry of

188

Finance, where we paid a tax of 30% of the total cost of the tickets ($900). Back to Air France to pay for and be issued our tickets. We were scheduled to leave on January 17, 1977. On to the Bank of Uganda where we showed our tickets and asked for $1000 in foreign currency. We explained that we were traveling with two small children. The officer never looked up or spoke. He crossed out $1000, wrote $200, stamped our papers and handed them back. We left, grateful to get anything. We were issued ten, twenty dollar travelers' checks. We were very close to freedom. It had taken us three years to get this all together, but we had done it, by the grace of God.

When we got back to Mbale, we started to make our final plans. We would only take two suitcases. The rest of our things would be left with Patrick. Our tickets said that we would leave from Entebbe, fly to Nairobi, Kenya and two days later leave for the United States. While in Nairobi we would get the necessary visas.

Then we heard some disturbing news about Entebbe. The military commander who must sign all exit papers was often not available or too drunk to function when his signature was needed. Also planes often overflew Entebbe because there are few passengers, no fuel and drunken soldiers with guns. Our only sure bet was to fly from Kenya. That would mean crossing the border by car and taking a bus to Nairobi. If the soldiers at the border found we had tickets to leave from Entebbe and we are going to Nairobi by road, they might think we are trying to hide something. They might even refuse to let us pass. We were so near and yet so far.

Our final plan was this. A friend in the Air Force, who knew most of the men at the border, would drive us across. We hid the airline tickets in the bottom of the suitcase. We hid the travelers' checks in Edwards's jacket pocket. We hoped they wouldn't search a small boy. We told the children not to say anything. "Don't tell them you're going to visit your Grandma and Grandpa in America. Don't talk about the plane. Don't talk."

Our official story was that we were going to Kitale, a town just across the Kenya border, to visit relatives. This was plausible because James' tribe is split right down the middle by the Kenya-Uganda border.

We could see the border post before we arrived. All trees and brush had been cleared for miles around to stop smugglers. There was one soldier visible sitting in front of the small building with a machine gun at this feet. He rose as we stopped the car. I stayed in the car with the children while James and our friend got out and greeted the soldier profusely. Another soldier came out of the building. He also knew our friend and they began talking.

The first solider asked James to open the trunk. He also told me to get out of the car. My heart was racing. I climbed out grasping the children by the hand, praying they would be silent. He opened the suitcases and searched them half heatedly. He briefly looked in the car and asked me where we are going. I replied, "Kitale." Once again he circled the car and peered inside. His eye fell on something. He reached into the car and removed something from the dashboard. What did he find? A hint? Some clue that we were not what we said, that we were not bound for Kitale?

The impulse to run and scream was almost overpowering. As he straightened up I saw what he had in his hand; a package of cigarettes. He put them in his pocket, walked back to his chair and lit one. I do not remember getting back in the car or going through the checkpoint on the Kenya side. We were half way to Kitale before my mind consciously functioned again. We were out, free, safe.

On January 20, 1977 we landed at Kennedy Airport in New York; tired, stiff, rumpled, happy, and sad. Escalators, highways, immigration, baggage, all went by in a haze. There was a small television on one of the ticket counters, and a peanut farmer from Georgia was being sworn in as President of the United States. Two impossible dreams came true on that day.

And I cried. I cried for James so far from home. I cried for me so happy to be home. I cried for our children, what they would have and what they would miss. I cried for Uganda, the shattered Pearl of Africa.

Epilogue

Idi Amin's government was overthrown in April, 1979 by liberators under the banner of the Uganda National Liberation Army (UNLA). Amin is now in exile in Saudi Arabia. Yusuf Lule, Godfrey Binaisa and Paul Mwanga each led Uganda for brief periods as new political alliances developed, collapsed and jockeyed for position.

In 1980 Milton Obote, who had been deposed by Amin, regained the presidency in a controversial election. Obote and his army set about a campaign of revenge. This reign of terror equaled Amin's in its ferocity and brutality.

Obote's government was also embroiled in a long guerrilla war with the National Resistance Army (NRA) led by Yoweri Museveni. Internal strife in Obote's army and lack of success against the NRA, led to Obote's second removal from power.

But the chaos continued under the next president, Major General Tito Okello, who was sworn in July of 1985. In January 1986, the NRA captured Kampala and Yoweri Museveni was sworn in as president.

In the past fifteen years, Uganda has undertaken the monumental task of rebuilding. Everything from the roads to the constitution had to be reconstructed.

Uganda also found itself in the throes of an AIDS epidemic. President Museveni openly acknowledged the problem and asked for help. With a program of education and awareness, the infection rate has dropped dramatically and Uganda has become the model for other African nations to follow in dealing with AIDS.

In 2001 there was an open, free, multi-party election and Yoweri Museveni was re-elected. The Pearl of Africa is regaining its luster.

> God Bless Africa
> Guard her people
> Guide her leaders
> And give her peace[2]

After leaving Uganda, we settled in Alabama. We lived with my parents who had moved there after retirement to escape the cold Chicago winters. James and I fought our way through the immigration maze, found work and were planning to move into our own home.

On July 29, 1978 James died in a traffic accident near Tuskegee, Alabama. As many times as I had thought about being widowed in Uganda, it had come upon me when least expected. But life would not allow me to

---

[2] Composed for people who wanted to pray for Africa quoted in an address at Nashotah House Episcopal Seminary, Nashotha, Wisconsin. April 22, 1966.

wallow in the sea of whys and what ifs for very long. There were children to raise, dreams to be dreamed, obstacles to overcome and battles to be fought. In fact, a situation was developing right in the small Alabama community where we lived.....but that's another story.

12803605R00115

Made in the USA
Charleston, SC
29 May 2012